CA

Vancouver

The Insider's Guide to Neighborhood Cafes

By Richard Wolak and Arthur Wolak

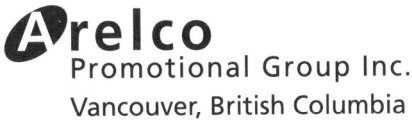

Arelco
Promotional Group Inc.
Vancouver, British Columbia

Copyright © 2001 by Arthur Wolak and Richard Wolak

All rights reserved. No part of this publication may be reproduced, transmitted, transcribed, photocopied, recorded, stored in a retrieval system, or translated without written permission of the publisher. Requests for permission should be made in writing to Arelco Promotional Group Inc., Post Office Box 2181, Vancouver, BC V5Y 2P8.

National Library of Canada Cataloguing-in-Publication Data

Wolak, Richard.

Cafes Vancouver : the insider's guide to neighborhood cafes

Includes index.
ISBN 0-9698040-1-6

1. Coffeehouses – British Columbia – Vancouver Metropolitan Area – Guidebooks. I. Wolak, Arthur. II. Title.

TX907.5.C22V354 2001   647.95711'33   C2001-901984-X

Distributed in Canada by:

Whitecap Books
170 Shields Court, Unit 2, Markham, ON L3R 9T5
Phone: (905) 470-8484 ext. 22, Fax: (905) 470-6787
Toll Free: 1-888-870-3442 ext. 22
whitecap@whitecap.ca

Cover and layout by Daylight Media
Maps by Fennana Design
Printed and bound in Canada

DISCLAIMER

Although great care has been taken in putting together this publication, and the contents are believed to be correct at press time, the authors and publisher of CAFES Vancouver hereby disclaim any liability for loss or damage resulting from omissions, misspellings, or errors, however caused, or for changes in details given in the guidebook, or for the consequences of any reliance on the information provided. Brand and product names are trademarks of their respective holders.

Published in Canada by
Arelco Promotional Group Inc.
Vancouver • www.arelco.com

Dedication

To our mother for her love of coffee and tea, and most of all for her encouragement.

Contents

List of Maps	vii
Acknowledgements	ix
Preface	xi
About The Authors	xiii
How to use this book	xv

Neighborhoods/Areas

Vancouver	
Downtown	7
West Side	35
East Side	65
West Vancouver	79
North Vancouver	83
Richmond	91
Delta	97
North Delta	
Ladner	
Tsawwassen	
Burnaby	103
Coquitlam	109
Surrey	115
White Rock	121
Langley	127
Whistler	133
Victoria	139

Day Trips

Mission	147
Abbotsford	147
Sidney	149
Salt Spring Island	150
Nanaimo	153
Campbell River	155

Contents

Theme Lists
Cafe Snacks	31
Late-Night Cafes	63
Internet Cafes	76
Breakfast Cafes	88
Chai Tea Cafes	100
Business-Meeting Cafes	107
Child-Friendly Cafes	113
Teahouses	124
Cafes on the Internet	137
Cafe Beverage Glossary	156
Coffee Roasters	159

Theme Index	165
Cafe Index	169
The Final word	173

List of Maps

Area	Map	Page Number
Overview	Map 1	2
Downtown Vancouver	Map 2	4
West Side	Map 3	32
East Side	Map 4	64
West Vancouver	Map 5	78
North Vancouver		
Richmond	Map 6	90
Delta		
North Delta		
Ladner		
Tsawwassen		
Burnaby	Map 7	102
Coquitlam	Map 8	108
Surrey	Map 9	114
White Rock		
Langley		
Whistler	Map 10	132
Victoria	Map 11	138
Mission	Map 12	146
Abbotsford		
Sidney	Map 13	148
Salt Spring Island		
Nanaimo	Map 14	152
Campbell River		

VII

Acknowledgements

For sharing their local insights we would like to thank Steve Feldman in Victoria, Wendy Kinnear in Whistler, Fiona Stuart in Nanaimo, and Deborah Wolfe in the Fraser Valley. Thanks also to the staff at Whitecap Books for their helpful suggestions, and to all the cafes and roasters who shared their knowledge about our region's cafe scene.

Preface

Greater Vancouver, famous for its friendly inhabitants, spectacular scenery, and damp weather, is also appreciated for its great cafes! However, if you've experienced a craving for a first-rate cup of coffee or tea, but couldn't decide on a place to get that particular thirst-quencher, you're not alone. The number of coffeehouses and teahouses has grown so fast in recent years that even experienced coffee and tea drinkers have been confounded by the variety of places around serving first-rate brews.

Cafes Vancouver has been designed not only to help discriminating coffee and tea drinkers who already appreciate the enticing, almost hypnotic aromas of freshly brewed coffee or tea—though it will certainly please them too!—but any coffee or tea drinker who wants some relief from the "instant" coffee brands and common tea bags lining the shelves of every grocery and convenience store.

Informative chapters consider cafe terminology and the region's coffee-bean-roasting companies. But the main focus is on the cafes—over two hundred locations presented in alphabetical order according to location where these fine flavours can be fully enjoyed. Specific names can also be looked up alphabetically and by theme in the indexes at the end of the book. Maps will help guide you to each destination.

Perhaps you'd like to know who makes the absolute "best" cup of coffee or tea. Well, you're not going to find out in this book since there is no definitive answer! Many factors—each liked or disliked to various degrees depending on one's tastes—affect the flavour. Some coffee considerations: the type of bean used, the particular roasting and grinding process, the brewing method, or even the glass or mug the resulting liquid is poured into! With the exception of roasting and grinding, the same applies to tea.

Preface

Since the assessment of any coffee or tea brew's quality is largely determined by one's individual preferences, prior experiences, expectations, and even a cafe's ambience, we do not offer a "rating scale" of any beverage served at locations contained in **Cafes Vancouver**. After all, whether you like your coffee or tea stronger or weaker, darker or brighter, sweeter or more bitter, it's ultimately your personal opinion that matters most.

Sampling lots of different beverages is the best way to find a personal favourite cafe. But don't over-indulge yourself! Too much of a good thing can spoil the pleasure (and possibly affect your health!). Moderation is the best approach to ensuring the continued enjoyment of virtually any food or beverage. It's worth pointing out that most places offer plenty of satisfying decaffeinated and herbal choices.

So, whether you crave a "quick jolt" of caffeine-laden espresso or just want a relaxing place to sip a coffee or tea, **Cafes Vancouver** will prove an invaluable resource for exploring the region's cafes and enjoying the many delicious flavours.

Arthur Wolak
and Richard Wolak

About The Authors

Richard Wolak is a well-known authority on the local and regional coffee scene. Since 1995, he has been vice president of sales and marketing for Arelco Promotional Group Inc., a marketing solutions company. Co-author of Vancouver's Best Espresso Spots and co-author of Oregon's Hot Java, Richard has been featured in many newspaper articles, including the Vancouver Sun, Vancouver Province, and The Oregonian. His media appearances include CBC Radio's Morning Show and BCTV News.

Arthur Wolak, president of Arelco Promotional Group Inc., has extensive marketing experience. After earning a BA from the University of British Columbia with a major in psychology, Arthur went on to complete graduate work in history and business, earning an MA from California State University and an MBA from the University of Colorado. Editor of Vancouver's Best Espresso Spots and co-author of Oregon's Hot Java, Arthur enjoys researching and writing whenever he has the time.

How To Use This Book

We have designed this book to help you navigate with ease among Greater Vancouver and regional cafes. Below is a primer on how to get the most from this guide and enhance your cafe experience.

CAFE LISTINGS

Each cafe's listing includes an address, phone number, "neighborhood," and a brief description of the site's features, typical clientele, and general ambience. Refer to "Cafes on the Internet" for places with an entertaining and informative presence on the Web.

Major coffee brands are noted where establishments have provided such information. Consult the "Directory of Coffee Bean Roasters" for some background on many of them complete with Web addresses for those who want to explore the topic in greater depth.

MAPS

Cafes are listed alphabetically by "neighborhood," and identified in a map at the beginning of each major geographical area. To locate a cafe on a map, simply note the map number and reference number on the left of the cafe's description, then flip to the specific neighborhood map and scan for the coffee cup marked with the number of the cafe. It's that simple!

THEME LISTS

Throughout the book there are useful "Theme Lists" of cafes for people with special interests, from teahouses, Internet cafes, breakfast cafes, late-night cafes, business-meeting cafes, to child-friendly cafes (where your kids should enjoy themselves as much as you!).

THEME INDEX

For cafes featuring entertainment that appeals to your interests, whether live music, art exhibitions, poetry, or author readings, check the Theme Index in the back for locations.

CAFES Vancouver

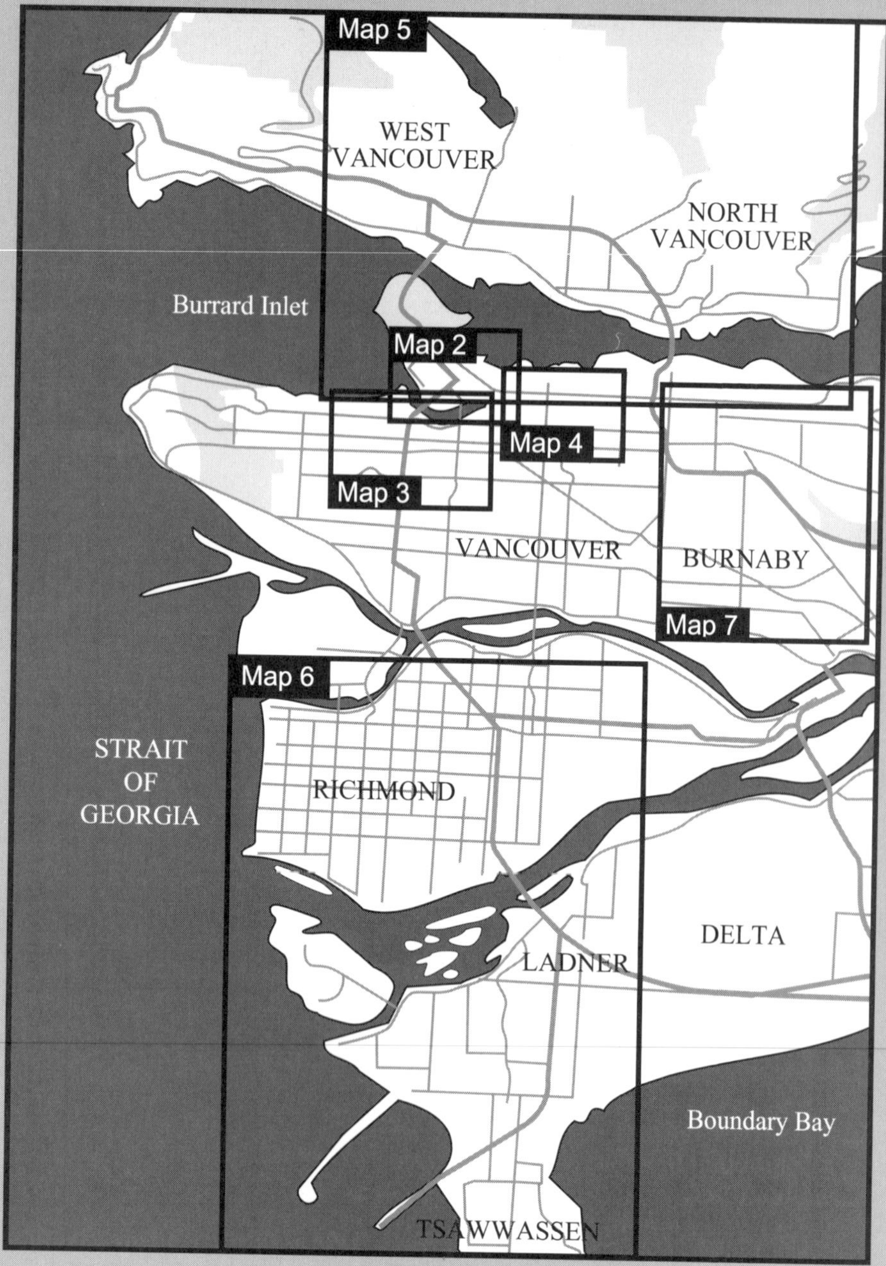
Map 5
WEST VANCOUVER
NORTH VANCOUVER
Burrard Inlet
Map 2
Map 4
Map 3
VANCOUVER
BURNABY
Map 7
Map 6
STRAIT OF GEORGIA
RICHMOND
DELTA
LADNER
Boundary Bay
TSAWWASSEN

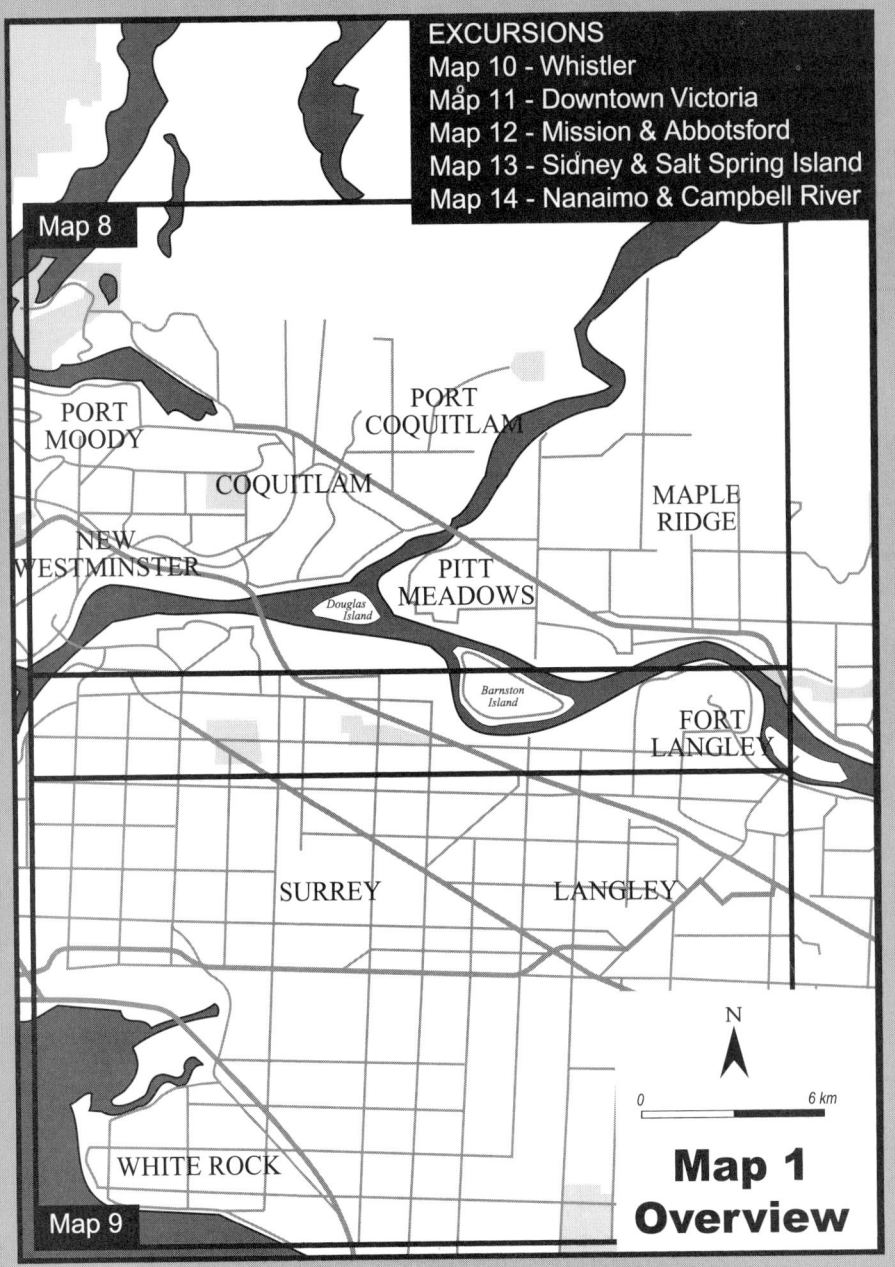

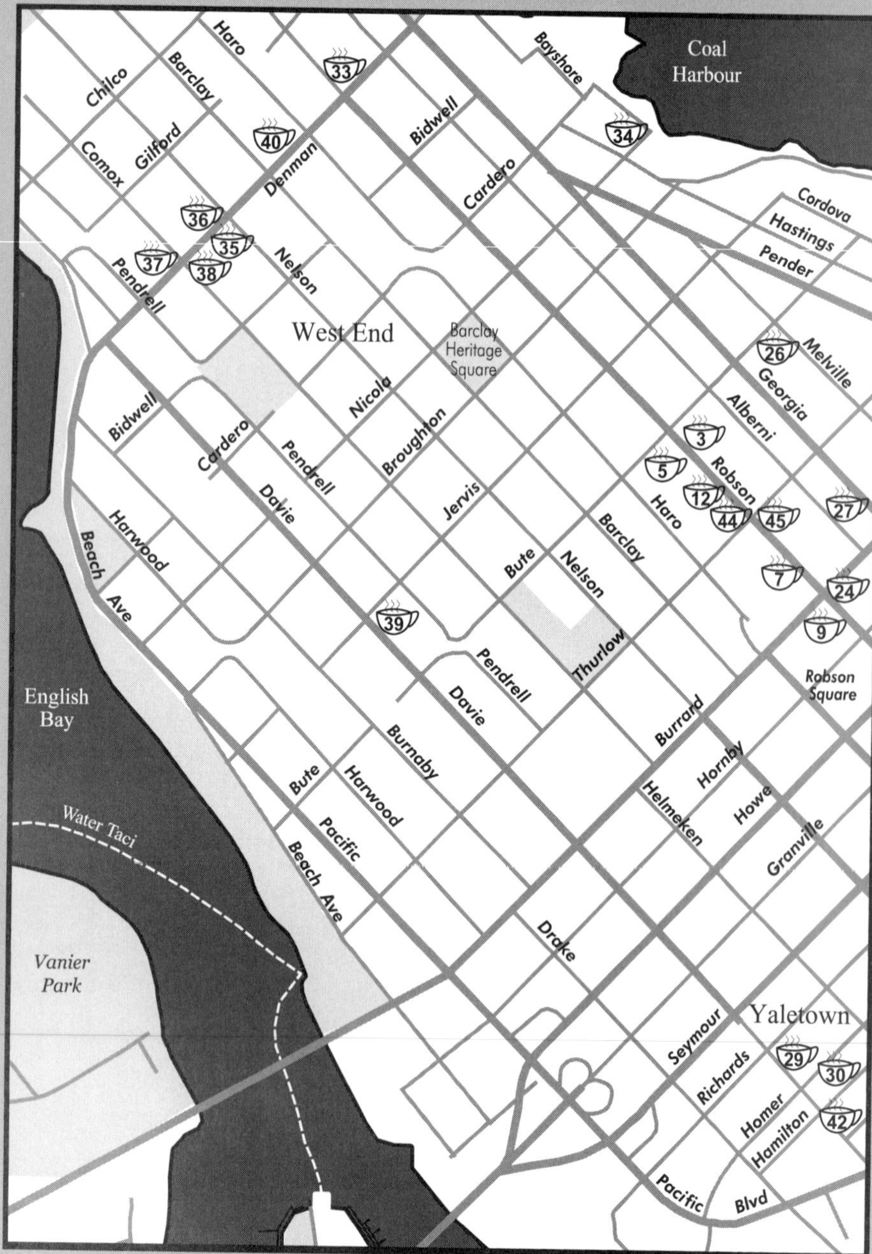
Coal Harbour
Haro
Barclay
Chilco
Comox
Gilford
33
40
Denman
Bidwell
Bayshore
34
Cardero
Cordova
Hastings
Pender
36
35
37
38
Pendrell
Nelson
West End
Barclay Heritage Square
26
Melville
Georgia
Alberni
Bidwell
Cardero
Nicola
Pendrell
Broughton
3
5
Robson
12
44
45
27
Davie
Jervis
Haro
Barclay
Harwood
Beach
Ave
Bute
Nelson
7
24
39
9
Thurlow
Pendrell
Robson Square
English Bay
Davie
Burrard
Burnaby
Bute
Harwood
Hornby
Helmeken
Howe
Water Taci
Pacific
Beach Ave
Granville
Drake
Vanier Park
Yaletown
Seymour
29
Richards
30
Homer
42
Hamilton
Pacific
Blvd

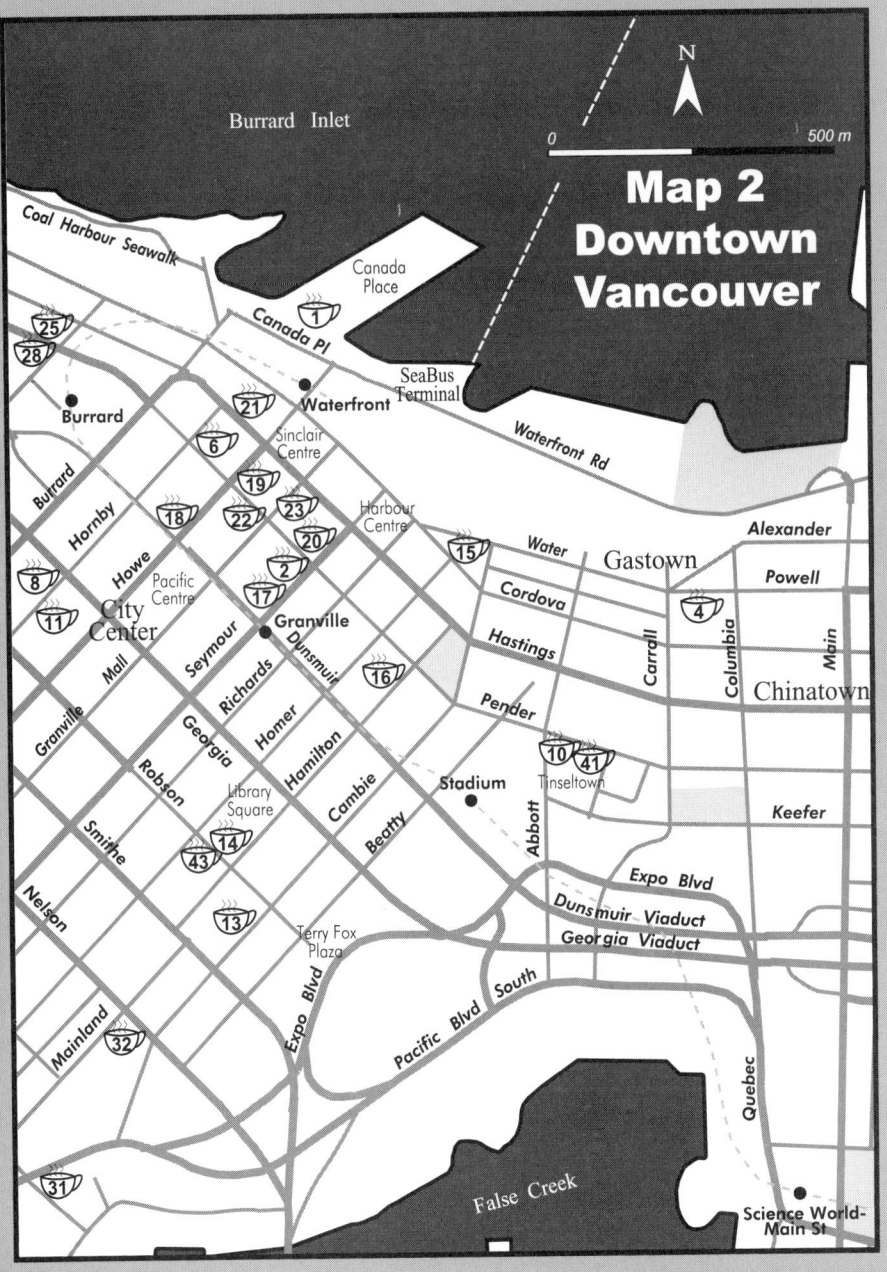

Downtown Vancouver

Tens of thousands of people work and live in the office towers and condos of Downtown Vancouver, a relatively small area of land surrounded by the waters of Burrard Inlet in the north, False Creek to the south and English Bay to the west. Within this area are many popular neighborhoods. Starting from the east is Gastown, historically the oldest part of the city known for its distinctive late Victorian architecture. In the south is Yaletown, a former warehouse quarter that has undergone rapid redevelopment as a high-rise residential and retail community. The West End, known for its many apartment buildings and as the entry point to Stanley Park, marks Downtown's western boundary. In central Downtown, the Financial District dominates West Hastings, Pender, and Georgia Streets, interspersed with busy cross streets such as Burrard, Thurlow and Bute. A focal point for both local shoppers and tourists is Robson Street, a distinctive Downtown "neighborhood" of its own. No matter which area you visit, in the listings that follow you'll find many great cafes.

Downtown Vancouver

Aromaz

140 - 999 Canada Place
DOWNTOWN
604-891-2555

Map: 2
Reference: 1
Hours: M-F 7am - 4:30pm
Coffee: Starbucks
Clientele: convention, business, and cruise ship tourists
Ambience: relaxing, open and airy

Inside the Pan Pacific Hotel right next to the cruise ship terminal, Aromaz is an upbeat and energetic cafe with friendly service and a popular outdoor patio. Food includes sandwiches, salads, lasagnas, cannelloni, hearty soups and a variety of desserts. You can also buy pre-packaged coffee beans, mints and chocolates to take home.

Big Dog Deli

523 Seymour Street
DOWNTOWN
604-684-9987

Map: 2
Reference: 2
Hours: M-F 7:30am - 6pm, Sat & Sun 11am - 5pm
Coffee: Seattle's Best Coffee
Clientele: business people, students and tourists
Ambience: comfortable and casual

Big Dog Deli is known as much for its coffee as its ambiance. As the name implies, walls are lined with photos of Big Dog customers and their canines. A nice feature if you love dogs and dog themes. If you're a cat person, no problem! Eat in, take out or call to have your coffees, grilled Italian panini sandwiches, wrapps, soups, salads and baked goods delivered right to your office. Big Dog also sells a variety of cooking oils, spices, teas and coffees.

Downtown Vancouver

Big Joe Coffee

1189 Robson Street
ROBSON
604-689-2470

Map: 2
Reference: 3
Hours: M-Th 7am - 9:30pm, F 7am - 10pm, Sat 7:30am - 10pm, Sun 8:30am - 8pm
Coffee: Premio d'Italia
Clientele: Robson Street shoppers and tourists
Ambience: cozy, warm and inviting

Have a drink on the outdoor patio and watch busy Robson Street shoppers walk by. You can also sit inside and enjoy some music and personalized service. Focaccia grilled sandwiches, pizza, soups, chili, ice cream, smoothies and mochacinos are always popular.

The Blinding Light Cinema & Cafe

36 Powell Street
GASTOWN
604-684-8288

Map: 2
Reference: 4
Hours: M 8:30am - 5:30pm, T-F 8:30am - 9:30pm, Sat & Sun 11:30am - 9:30pm
Coffee: Torrefazione Italia
Clientele: neighborhood and independent cinema fans
Ambience: relaxed and nice

Located on the southern edge of Gastown, this cafe is part of the Blinding Light Cinema, which showcases independent films. So, before or after a movie, enjoy a coffee or a bite to eat. The Blinding Light Cafe serves spinach-feta samosas, salads, wrapps, and freshly baked goods.

Downtown Vancouver

Bojangles Café

785 Denman Street
WEST END
604-687-3622

Map: 2
Reference: 33
Hours: M-Th 6am - 11pm, F & Sat 6am - 12am, Sun 7am - 11pm
Coffee: JJ Bean
Clientele: locals and tourists
Ambience: cozy and casual

In the heart of the West End, this cafe is an ideal place to enjoy a light meal. A selection of fine coffees, baked goods, sandwiches, and soups are available inside or on the patio outside. At Bojangles on Denman sandwiches have unique names such as the "Turkey Orleans," "Royal Street Smoked Salmon," and the "Dixieland Veggie Delight." One of the most popular beverages is the "Chaipuccino"—chai blended with steamed milk and topped with light foam.

Bojangles on the Waterfront

1506 Coal Harbour Way
WEST END
604-687-6599

Map: 2
Reference: 34
Hours: M-F 7am - 8pm, Sat & Sun 8am - 8pm
Coffee: JJ Bean
Clientele: locals and tourists
Ambience: bright and relaxing

Bojangles at Coal Harbour has a great view of Stanley Park and the North Shore and is an ideal place to take a break from your busy routine and watch boats sailing by. Named in tribute to the New Orleans Jazz dancer and musician "Bojangles," experience some great jazz while enjoying fine coffees, teas and freshly baked goods, sandwiches, soups and Italian ice creams. A breakfast menu is available.

Downtown Vancouver

Bread Garden Bakery & Cafe

1040 Denman Street
WEST END
604-685-2996

Map: 2
Reference: 35
Hours: M-Th 6am - 12am,
F & Sat 6am - 2am,
Sun 6am - 12am
Coffee: JJ Bean
Clientele: West End residents, shoppers, and tourists
Ambience: cozy and comfortable

The Bread Garden offers a large selection of high quality fresh foods and beverages at three downtown locations. The menu includes roasted vegetable lasagna, smoked salmon quiche, noodles & cheese, and "big bowls," such as the Curry Masala and Red Lentil Dahl. There are also a variety of wrapps, sandwiches, salads, and soups. Try the signature Cinnamon Knot, mango cheesecake, or chocolate macadamia pecan pie.

Bread Garden Bakery & Cafe

889 West Pender Street
DOWNTOWN
604-638-3982

Map: 2
Reference: 6
Hours: M-F 6am - 6pm, closed Sat & Sun
Coffee: JJ Bean
Clientele: businesspeople, shoppers, and tourists
Ambience: cozy and comfortable

Downtown Vancouver

Bread Garden Bakery & Cafe

812 Bute Street
ROBSON
604-688-3213

Map: 2
Reference: 5
Hours: M-Th 6am - 2am,
F & Sat 6am - 3am,
Sun 6am - 2am
Coffee: JJ Bean
Clientele: West End residents, shoppers, and tourists
Ambience: cozy and comfortable

See previous entry for details.

Café Crepe

1032 Robson Street
ROBSON
604-488-0045

Map: 2
Reference: 7
Hours: M-Th 8am - 11pm,
F & Sat 8am - 12am,
Sun 8am - 11pm
Coffee: Illy
Clientele: businesspeople, shoppers and tourists
Ambience: Parisian style

Dine-in or take-out from Café Crepe, a Parisian-inspired cafe known for its great food, coffee, upbeat music, and warm and inviting decor. Savory and desert crepes are prepared in front of your eyes. Ementhal Cheese & Tuna, Nutella with Banana, Maple Syrup and Lemon Sugar are some of the most popular fillings. Specialty crepes feature your choice of liqueur and ice cream. Baguettes and panini sandwiches, which are grilled, round off the menu. Try one of the special coffees or cold drinks.

Downtown Vancouver

Caffe Artigiano

1101 West Pender Street
FINANCIAL DISTRICT
604-685-5333

Map: 2
Reference: 25
Hours: M-F 5:30am - 5pm, Sat 6:30am - 4pm, Sun closed
Coffee: Caffe Vita
Clientele: business district, tourists
Ambience: Florentine, Tuscan

Experience authentic Italian ambiance without leaving the city. Enjoy homemade Italian panini sandwiches, soups, salads, breakfast items, and sweets while reading the paper and listening to music at Caffe Artigiano, a warm and inviting establishment that elevates coffee to an art form. Highly skilled baristas top off lattes, cappuccinos and Macchiatos with unique milk-foam designs. The espresso machine uses a two-drip spout so each espresso becomes a double shot for the price of a single.

Canadian Maple Delights

769 Hornby Street
DOWNTOWN
604-682-6175

Map: 2
Reference: 8
Hours: M-F 7:30am - 7pm, Sat & Sun 8am - 7pm
Coffee: Crown
Clientele: French Canadians, office workers, convention visitors, and tourists
Ambience: comfortable

At Canadian Maple Delights everything has a hint of Maple. Crepes, pancakes, maple quesadillas and maple chicken curry salad are sought after items on the breakfast, lunch and dinner menu. Enjoy gourmet soups, salads, sandwiches, ice cream and desserts, each enhanced with the subtle, rich flavor of maple. Maple syrup, maple vinaigrette, maple spread and maple mustard are some unique items that can be found on the shelves. The ice maple latte and hot maple lemon tea are crowd favourites.

Downtown Vancouver

Citrus Café

644 Bute Street
FINANCIAL DISTRICT
604-682-2068

Map: 2
Reference: 26
Hours: M-F 7am - 5pm, Sat & Sun closed
Coffee: Torrefazione Italia
Clientele: businesspeople
Ambience: relaxing and upbeat

At the Citrus Café patrons can sit along the spacious window looking at the view while enjoying homemade food and hot coffee. Tortilla pie, cinnamon buns and panini sandwiches are among the many popular menu items. Citrus Café also provides a catering service to local offices.

Coo Coo Coffee

477 Davie Street
YALETOWN
604-605-0938

Map: 2
Reference: 29
Hours: M-F 6am - 6pm, Sat & Sun 9am - 5pm
Coffee: Torrefazione Italia
Clientele: office workers and locals
Ambience: neighborhood coffee shop

At the edge of Yaletown, this small, cozy coffee shop with fireplace and heated outdoor patio offers personal service. Besides the wide assortment of beverages, Coo Coo Coffee will customize non-alcoholic beverages to meet your discerning tastes. A fine selection of pastries, sandwiches and Italian ice cream is served.

Downtown Vancouver

Death By Chocolate

1001 Denman Street
WEST END
604-899-2462

Map: 2
Reference: 36
Hours: M-Th 8am - 12am, F & Sat 8am - 1am, Sun 8am - 12am
Coffee: Seattle's Best Coffee
Clientele: chocolate and ice cream fans and coffee connoisseurs
Ambience: art deco

At Death By Chocolate, on Robson and in the West End, the presentation is part of the experience. Watch expert pastry chefs create one of the thirty unique 'custom-designed' dessert creations. A few of the most popular include "Between The Sheets," "Latin Lover," "Ebony & Ivory," "Multitude Of Sins" and "Crumble In My Arms." There is a long list of sandwiches and baked goods, such as muffins, cookies, and dessert bars, and many espresso drinks from which to choose.

Death By Chocolate

818 Burrard Street
ROBSON
604-688-8234

Map: 2
Reference: 9
Hours: M-Th 7am - 12am, F 7am - 1am, Sat 11am - 1am, Sun 11am - 12am
Coffee: Seattle's Best Coffee
Clientele: chocolate & ice cream fans and coffee connoisseurs
Ambience: art deco

Downtown Vancouver

Death By Chocolate Express

2025 - 88 West Pender Street
DOWNTOWN
604-633-2364

Map: 2
Reference: 10
Hours: M-Sun 11am - 12am
Coffee: Seattle's Best Coffee
Clientele: chocolate & ice cream fans and moviegoers
Ambience: part of a food fair

Inside the Tinseltown shopping mall on the edge of Chinatown, there's something for everyone at Death By Chocolate Express. Selections include cakes, pies, cookies, ice cream, milkshakes, and coffees. Before or after a movie, drop by and satisfy your sweet tooth.

Delany's On Denman

1105 Denman Street
WEST END
604-662-3344

Map: 2
Reference: 37
Hours: M-Sun 6am - 12am
Coffee: JJ Bean
Clientele: eclectic and fun group of locals
Ambience: old style, classic coffeehouse

Near English Bay, this neighborhood meeting place is full from morning till night. At Delany's, a 2nd shot of espresso is added at no extra charge, only if you wish to have the "caffeine charge" of a 2nd shot! It's your choice. Lots of seating inside and out with newspapers and magazines for reading. Large selection of muffins, scones, cinnamon buns, cookies, biscotti, brownies, pies, cakes and sandwiches complement the beverage selection, which includes mochas with chocolate whip cream, cappuccinos, and lattes.

Downtown Vancouver

Gallery Café

750 Hornby Street
DOWNTOWN
604-688-2233

Map: 2
Reference: 11
Hours: M-Sat 9am - 5pm, Sun 10am - 5pm
Coffee: JJ Bean
Clientele: businesspeople and art gallery patrons
Ambience: classical elegance

Located within the Vancouver Art Gallery, Gallery Café has a large indoor seating area and outdoor patio to enjoy on a beautiful sunny day. Homemade foods include a variety of hot entrees, quiches, salads, and sandwiches, including fresh roasted turkey, shrimp salad, roast beef, and roasted vegetable. Desserts complement the large variety of hot and cold beverages. Gallery Café also does catering with advanced notice.

Ghirardelli Soda Fountain & Chocolate Shop

1132 Robson Street
ROBSON
604-688-9929

Map: 2
Reference: 12
Hours: M-Th 11am - 10pm, F & Sat 11am - 11pm, Sun 11am - 10pm
Coffee: Blenz
Clientele: locals and tourists
Ambience: 1950's "Soda Fountain"

Originating in San Francisco in 1852 just around the time of the gold rush, Ghiradelli remains among the oldest chocolate-making companies in North America. Vancouver's location is the only one operating outside of the USA. A fun shop filled with chocolate bars and seasonal gifts, Ghirardelli specializes in old-fashioned ice-cream sodas and sundaes. Espresso ice cream is a popular choice.

Downtown Vancouver

Grounds For Appeal

845 Cambie Street
DOWNTOWN
Phone 604-681-8558

Map: 2
Reference: 13
Hours: M-F 7am - 4:30pm, Sat & Sun closed
Coffee: Seattle's Best Coffee
Clientele: office workers and students
Ambience: busy yet casual

Located inside the Law Society building, Grounds For Appeal has a diverse menu with something for everyone, from sandwiches, salads, pizza, lasagna, chow mein and burritos to a wide assortment of desserts and pastries. The spacious inside courtyard is ideal for group lunches and meetings.

Guttenberg's Café

345 Robson Street
LIBRARY SQUARE
604-669-4452

Map: 2
Reference: 14
Hours: M-F 6am - 6pm, Sat 8am - 4pm, Sun closed
Coffee: House Blend
Clientele: office workers, library visitors, locals and tourists
Ambience: European style

Close to BC Place and Yaletown, Gutenberg's is a Robson-Street fixture situated next to the main branch of the Vancouver Public Library. The cafe offers a classic European ambience with a wide selection of pastries, sandwiches, coffees and teas. Drop by on the way to or from the library and read a book while enjoying a refreshing beverage or snack.

Downtown Vancouver

Hole In The Wall Cappuccino Bar

135 - 1030 West Georgia Street
FINANCIAL DISTRICT
604-646-4653

Map: 2
Reference: 27
Hours: M-F 7am - 4pm, Sat & Sun closed
Coffee: Canterbury
Clientele: business professionals, students and tourists
Ambience: warm, friendly, upbeat

As with any "hole in the wall," this one is hard to find, but it's one worth finding! There's no direct street access. Enter this cafe via the Burrard Building lobby where you will find a variety of salads, baked products, panini sandwiches, and made-to-order breakfast bagel sandwiches for eat-in or take-out. There are televisions for the latest stock quotes, news, or sports events and a great selection of music.

Java Cat Coffee

401 West Cordova Street
GASTOWN
604-682-4037

Map: 2
Reference: 15
Hours: M-F 7am - 5pm, Sat 9am - 5pm, Sun closed
Coffee: House Blend
Clientele: office workers
Ambience: relaxed and casual

This hip, friendly cafe at the edge of Gastown near SFU Harbour Centre offers a place to relax while listening to progressive music and drinking a hot or cold beverage. Java Cat's in-house bakery produces a daily variety of muffins, breads, cinnamon buns, scones and cookies.

Downtown Vancouver

Java Cat Coffee

515 Hamilton Street
DOWNTOWN
604-682-4037

Map: 2
Reference: 16
Hours: M-F 7am - 5pm, Sat 9am - 5pm, Sun closed
Coffee: House Blend
Clientele: office workers and students
Ambience: relaxed and casual

Java Cat has a second location down the street from BC Hydro, close to Vancouver Community College, which offers the same food, beverages and music in a spacious facility.

Lingo Cyberbistro

547 Seymour Street
DOWNTOWN
604-331-9345

Map: 2
Reference: 17
Hours: M-F 7am - 7pm, Sat 8am - 4pm, Sun closed
Coffee: Torrefazione Italia
Clientele: office workers, shoppers, tourists and students
Ambience: casual

Located near the Seymour BCIT campus, this huge Internet cafe features fast Web access, and fresh, high quality baked treats, soups, salads, paninis, burritos, and a large selection of sandwiches, including the specialty of the house—the Montreal smoked meat sandwich. Beverages include coffee frappes, fruit smoothies, and other cold and hot drinks. Sit inside or order take out. Lingo Cyberbistro provides catering to local offices.

Downtown Vancouver

Mario's Coffee Express

595 Howe Street
DOWNTOWN
604-608-2804

Map: 2
Reference: 18
Hours: M-Th 7am - 5pm,
F 7am - 4pm, Sat & Sun closed
Coffee: House Blend
Clientele: office workers, tourists, and celebrities
Ambience: European

Latin music and warm decor characterize this Italian espresso bar. Many baked goods, biscottis, and desserts are on the menu as well as a variety of vegetarian and non-vegetarian panini and bagette sandwiches. Besides great food, beverages, and ambiance, Mario's is also known for its frequent celebrity sightings. Try the house special chai lattes.

Mondo Gelato

1094 Denman Street
WEST END
604-647-6638

Map: 2
Reference: 38
Hours: M-Sun, 9am - 12am
Coffee: Torrefazione Italia
Clientele: locals and tourists
Ambience: trendy

Serving Italian gelato freshly made each day on the premises, Mondo Gelato is more than just a place for ice cream. Try some unique items including Sorbetto (non-dairy, non-fat, fruit ice cream), Soya Gelato (sugar-free and cholesterol-free) and Gelato-non-Gelato (creamy chilled whipped milk). Ice cream cakes are always available. For a strong flavoured gelato, try the Espresso Affogato, a double shot of espresso poured over a scoop of vanilla ice cream. Other popular choices include the Nutella, Coconut or Mango ice cream. Fine coffees, teas and baked goods will complement any gelato choice.

Downtown Vancouver

Moon Beans Coffee Café

1285 Davie Street
WEST END
604-632-0032

Map: 2
Reference: 39
Hours: M-Th 7am - 11pm, F & S 7am - 12am, Sun 7am - 11pm
Coffee: House Blend
Clientele: West End community
Ambience: relaxed, fun and casual

Not far from English Bay, Moon Beans is a local meeting place that features a variety of menu items for breakfast, lunch and dinner. Desserts complement the beverage selections. There are lots of seats inside and a great patio.

Downtown Vancouver

Moonpennies

103 - 1112 West Pender Street
FINANCIAL DISTRICT
604-669-6092

Map: 2
Reference: 28
Hours: M-F 6am - 6pm, Sat & Sun 7am - 4pm
Coffee: Bean Around The World
Clientele: office workers and tourists
Ambience: cheerful and happy

Bustling with office workers during business hours, this popular cafe located close to the US Consulate, financial district and hotels provides a large indoor seating area. Moonpennies' menu includes a wide selection of homemade fresh gourmet baguette sandwiches, deli salads, soups, baked goods, and desserts. The breakfast menu includes omelettes and frittatas. For a coffee, why not try a "Moonpuccino" since you won't find one anywhere else except at Moonpennies.

Moonpennies

456 Howe Street
DOWNTOWN
604-899-1271

Map: 2
Reference: 19
Hours: M-F 6am - 6pm, Sat & Sun 7am - 4pm
Coffee: Bean Around The World
Clientele: office workers and tourists
Ambience: cheerful and happy

See above for description.

Downtown Vancouver

Mum's Gelati

855 Denman Street
WEST END
604-681-1500

Map: 2
Reference: 40
Hours: M-Sat 7:30am - 12am, Sun 8am - 12am
Coffee: Coliera
Clientele: locals and tourists
Ambience: rustic

Since 1973, Mum's Gelati has been serving homemade Italian ice cream and freshly baked goods. On a cone or in a cup, try the spumoni, mocha chip gelato or one of the picturesque lattes or cappuccinos. Gift certificates are available.

Pia's Classic Kaffe

605 West Pender Street
DOWNTOWN
604-684-2737

Map: 2
Reference: 20
Hours: M-F 7:30am - 6pm, Sat 11am - 5pm, Sun closed
Coffee: Café Classics
Clientele: businesspeople and students
Ambience: casual

In the same location for over 24 years, Pia's Classic Kaffe is the place to go for Scandinavian coffee and food. The menu includes soup, sandwiches, and pastries. Look for the daily coffee specials.

Downtown Vancouver

Portfolio Coffee Bar

863 West Hastings Street
DOWNTOWN
604-801-6928

Map: 2
Reference: 21
Hours: M-F 7am - 5pm, Sat & Sun closed
Coffee: Torrefazione Italia
Clientele: office workers, locals and tourists
Ambience: elegant and tranquil

With a view of the North Shore on the right, and the City Centre on the left, Portfolio Coffee Bar is an ideal spot to take a break from the office and enjoy fine coffees, teas, baked goods, paninis, soups and salads. This is not only a cafe but it's also an art gallery specializing in British Columbian fine glass and ceramic art. On a sunny day, you can't beat the patio.

Seattle's Best Coffee

1137 Hamilton Street
YALETOWN
604-685-6511

Map: 2
Reference: 30
Hours: M-F 6:30am - 7:30pm, Sat 7:30am - 7pm, Sun 7:30am - 6pm
Coffee: Seattle's Best Coffee
Clientele: eclectic business and residential community
Ambience: warm

This cafe, a local representative of the well-known American coffee chain, occupies a recently restored brick building in the heart of Yaletown. Custom-roasted coffee beans come from the company's roasting plant in Seattle and can be purchased by the pound as well as enjoyed, freshly brewed, on site. "Henry's Choice" coffee blend is popular. For an extra jolt, add a 2nd shot of espresso to any of the espresso-based beverages for no additional cost. A selection of freshly baked goods, including cookies and muffins, are always available.

Downtown Vancouver

Starbucks

88 West Pender Street
DOWNTOWN @ Tinseltown
604-687-6116

Map: 2
Reference: 41
Hours: M-F 6am - 10pm, Sat 7am - 10pm, Sun 7:30am - 9pm
Coffee: Starbucks
Clientele: shoppers
Ambience: comfortable and upbeat

Located in Tinseltown Mall near Chinatown, this spacious cafe offers all of Starbucks' trademark coffee and tea blends. Among the most popular are the "Frappuccino," a creamy, low-fat blend of coffee, milk, and other flavours customized with your choice of mocha, espresso, caramel or syrups. The "Latte Macchiato" has steamed milk topped with foam and marked with a ristretto shot ("short pull") poured through the centre of the drink. Food selection includes sandwiches, baked goods and desserts.

Starbucks

398 Robson Street
DOWNTOWN
604-687-1187

Map: 2
Reference: 43
Hours: M-W 5:30am - 8pm, Th & F 5:30am - 9pm, Sat 8:30 - 6pm, & Sun 10:30am - 6:00pm
Coffee: Starbucks
Clientele: businesspeople and locals
Ambience: comfortable and upbeat

Located at Library Square at Robson and Homer. See above for description.

Downtown Vancouver

Starbucks

1100 Robson Street
ROBSON
604-685-7991

Map: 2
Reference: 44
Hours: M-W 5:30am - 8pm, Th & F 5:30am - 9pm, Sat 8:30 - 6pm, & Sun 10:30am - 6:00pm
Coffee: Starbucks
Clientele: businesspeople and tourists
Ambience: comfortable and upbeat

Located at the corner of Robson and Thurlow. See previous Starbucks' description for details.

Starbucks

1099 Robson Street
ROBSON
604-685-1099

Map: 2
Reference: 45
Hours: M-W 5:30am - 8pm, Th & F 5:30am - 9pm, Sat 8:30 - 6pm, & Sun 10:30am - 6:00pm
Coffee: Starbucks
Clientele: businesspeople and tourists
Ambience: comfortable and upbeat

Located at the other corner of Robson and Thurlow. See previous Starbucks' description for details.

Downtown Vancouver

Starbucks

700 West Pender Street
DOWNTOWN
604-685-7373

Map: 2
Reference: 22
Hours: M-W 5:30am - 8pm, Th & F 5:30am - 9pm, Sat 8:30 - 6pm, & Sun 10:30am - 6:00pm
Coffee: Starbucks
Clientele: businesspeople and students
Ambience: comfortable and upbeat

Located on the north entrance of the Pacific Centre Mall, this spacious cafe offers all of Starbucks' trademark coffee and tea blends. Among the most popular are the "Frappuccino," a creamy, low-fat blend of coffee, milk, and other flavours customized with your choice of mocha, espresso, caramel or syrups. The "Latte Macchiato" has steamed milk topped with foam and marked with a ristretto shot ("short pull") poured through the centre of the drink. Food selection includes sandwiches, baked goods and desserts.

Starbucks

1195 Mainland Street
YALETOWN
604-662-4030

Map: 2
Reference: 42
Hours: M-Th 6am - 10pm, F & Sat 6am - 10:30pm, Sun 6am - 9:30pm
Coffee: Starbucks
Clientele: everyone
Ambience: casual, warm, inviting

Located at Mainland and Davie, this cafe offers all of Starbucks' trademark coffee and tea blends. Among the most popular are the "Caffe Mocha," a mix of mocha syrup and espresso with steamed milk topped off with whipped cream, and the "Cappuccino," the classic European-inspired beverage that contains a shot of espresso blended with steamed milk, capped by a layer of creamy foam. Food selection includes sandwiches, baked goods and desserts.

Downtown Vancouver

Trees Organic Coffee

450 Granville Street
DOWNTOWN
604-684-5060

Map: 2
Reference: 23
Hours: M-F 6am - 9pm, Sat 6am - 7pm, Sun 6am - 6pm
Coffee: Trees Organic
Clientele: business workers and students
Ambience: funky and homey

Trees Gourmet Coffee roasts its own organic coffee beans in small batches for fresh, natural flavours. Complementing the coffee and other beverages is a menu full of sandwiches, home-baked muffins, scones, cakes, and breads. Trees hosts SFU Harbour Centre's popular "Philosophers' Café" the last Wednesday of each month. Trees' own brand of coffee beans is available for wholesale and retail purchase.

Urban Fare

177 Davie Street
YALETOWN
604-975-7550

Map: 2
Reference: 31
Hours: M-Sun 6am - 12am
Coffee: JJ Bean
Clientele: urban professionals and locals
Ambience: bright and open

A great place for people watching, the coffee bar at the front of the huge Urban Fare gourmet grocery store features a variety of espresso drinks, teas, and baked goods. Try the Espresso Affogato. It's a double shot of espresso poured over a scoop of vanilla gelato. Have a muffin, scone, sandwich, soup, salad, sushi or something from the extensive selection of daily hot and cold food items. The grocery store is filled with French, English, and Italian imports. There's also a selection of cookbooks, newspapers and flowers.

Downtown Vancouver

Virgin Megastore Cafe

788 Burrard Street
ROBSON
604-669-2289

Map: 2
Reference: 24
Hours: M-Th 10am - 8pm, F 10am - 11pm, Sat 9am - 11pm, Sun 10am - 8pm
Coffee: Torrefazione Italia
Clientele: music lovers
Ambience: earthy atmosphere

In the heart of Vancouver's downtown shopping district, Virgin Megastore Cafe is located, as the name suggests, within Virgin Records at the corner of Robson and Burrard Streets. Formerly the site of Vancouver's original Main Public Library, this unique building has over three levels of music, books, video and other entertainment products. But don't forget to visit the 2nd floor where you can relax at the Virgin Cafe and enjoy one of the specialty coffees and pastries.

Yaletown Market

1002 Mainland Street
YALETOWN
604-685-9929

Map: 2
Reference: 32
Hours: M-F 8am - 6pm, Sat 9am - 5pm, Sun closed
Coffee: Bean Around The World
Clientele: office workers, computer techies, students
Ambience: hip and funky

Yaletown Market features a variety of coffees, teas, cold beverages and a huge selection of hot and cold sandwiches, soups, salads, samosas, wrapps, Jamaican rotis, cakes and cookies. The grocery store and market is filled with a large selection of dairy products, canned and dry goods. Yaletown Market is always packed at lunchtime with neighborhood regulars.

Cafe Snacks

While the variety and flavours may differ from cafe to cafe, there are some common—and less common, but still delicious and worthwhile!—snacks on espresso bar menus. The following are some definitions of foods carried by establishments in CAFES Vancouver.

BABKA - a rich sweet coffeecake baked with a variety of sweet fillings.

BAGEL - a donut-shaped roll with a tough, chewy, tasty texture, made from dough that is quickly boiled then baked.

BISCOTTI - crispy, crunchy Italian cookies great for dipping in coffee!

GELATO - Italian ice cream.

KNISH - potato and onion, among other fillings, stuffed in thin dough and baked. An East European treat!

LATKE - fried grated-potato pancakes, often with a hint of onion for extra flavour.

PANINI - Italian sandwiches, grilled or cold, made with such fillings as vegetables, cheese, and meat.

RUGELACH - bite-size chocolate and/or fruit-filled pastry.

SAMOSA - mixture of potatoes, peas, carrots and Indian spices, ground up and stuffed in pastry and fried until done.

SCONES - small, rich, biscuit-like pastries baked in an oven or on a griddle. They're famous culinary exports from Britain!

WRAPPS - tortillas wrapped around a variety of fillings.

Map 3
West Side

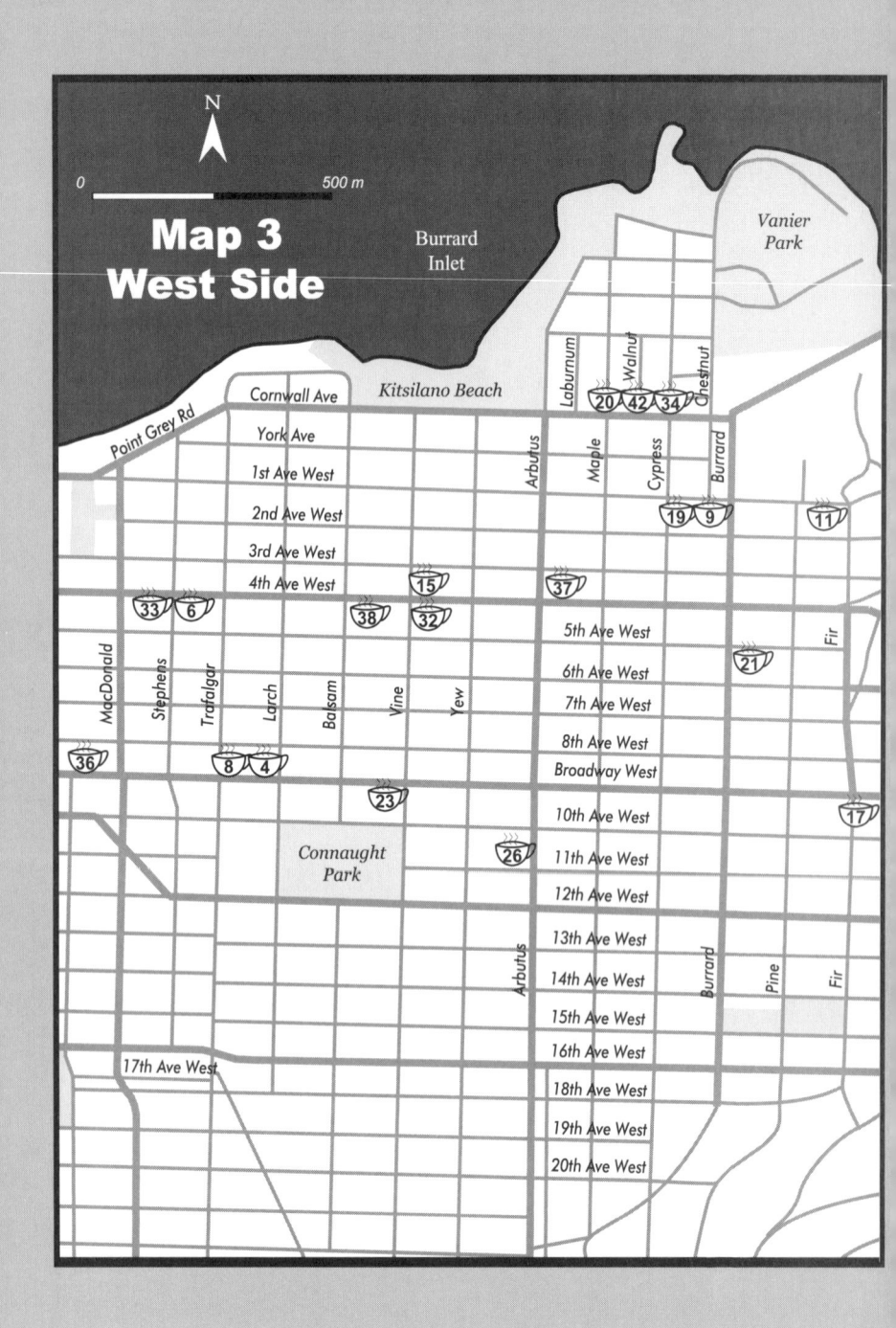

Burrard Inlet

Vanier Park

Point Grey Rd

Cornwall Ave

Kitsilano Beach

York Ave
1st Ave West
2nd Ave West
3rd Ave West
4th Ave West
5th Ave West
6th Ave West
7th Ave West
8th Ave West
Broadway West
10th Ave West
11th Ave West
12th Ave West
13th Ave West
14th Ave West
15th Ave West
16th Ave West
17th Ave West
18th Ave West
19th Ave West
20th Ave West

Laburnum, Walnut, Chestnut, Arbutus, Maple, Cypress, Burrard, Fir, Pine

MacDonald, Stephens, Trafalgar, Larch, Balsam, Vine, Yew

Connaught Park

20, 42, 34, 19, 9, 11, 33, 6, 15, 38, 32, 37, 21, 36, 8, 4, 23, 26, 17

32

Map

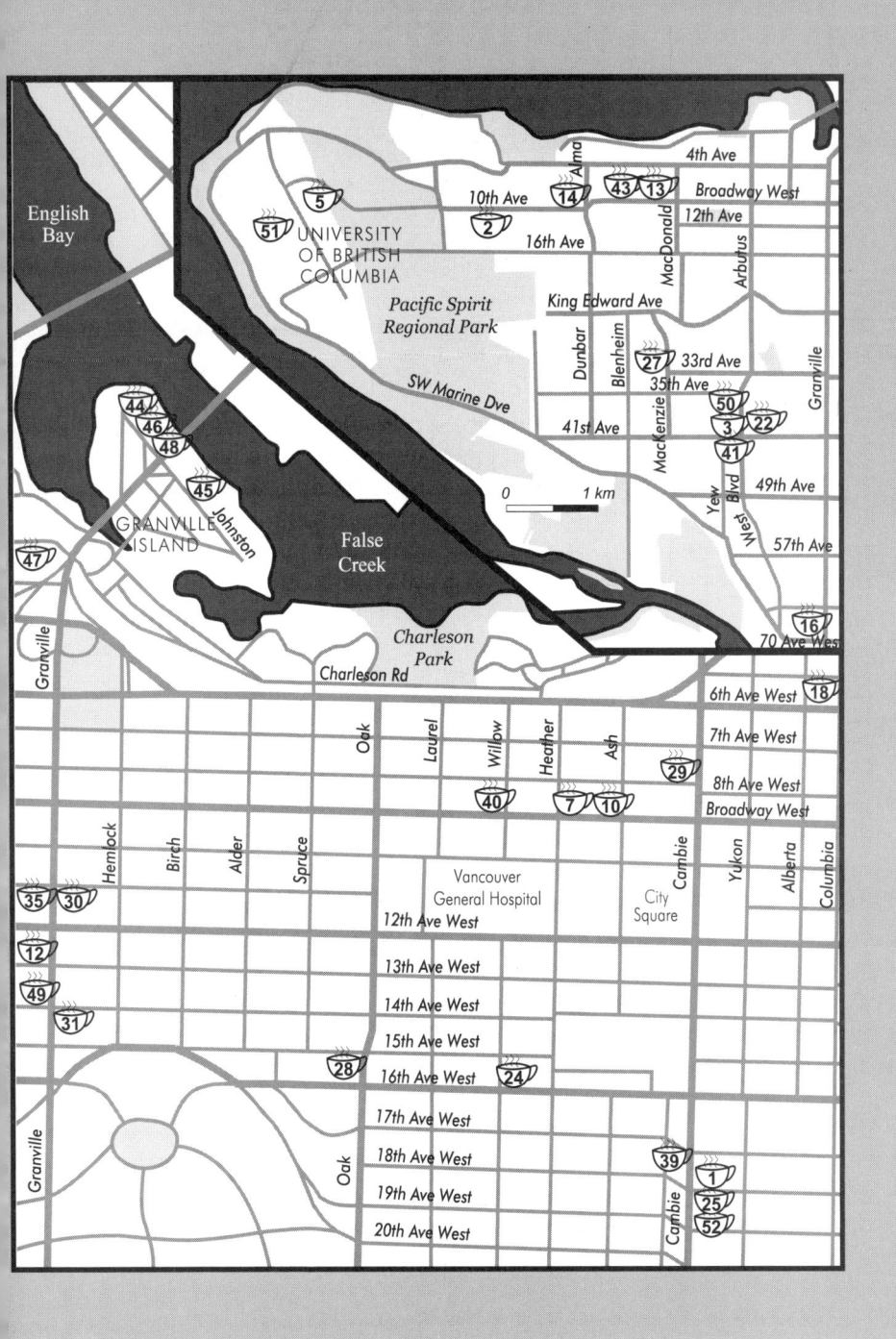

English Bay

University of British Columbia

Pacific Spirit Regional Park

Granville Island

False Creek

Charleson Park

Vancouver General Hospital

City Square

Streets and avenues:
- 4th Ave
- Broadway West
- 10th Ave
- 12th Ave
- 16th Ave
- King Edward Ave
- SW Marine Dve
- 33rd Ave
- 35th Ave
- 41st Ave
- 49th Ave
- 57th Ave
- 70 Ave West
- 6th Ave West
- 7th Ave West
- 8th Ave West
- Broadway West
- Charleson Rd
- 12th Ave West
- 13th Ave West
- 14th Ave West
- 15th Ave West
- 16th Ave West
- 17th Ave West
- 18th Ave West
- 19th Ave West
- 20th Ave West

Cross streets: Alma, MacDonald, Arbutus, Dunbar, Blenheim, Mackenzie, Granville, Yew, West Blvd, Oak, Laurel, Willow, Heather, Ash, Cambie, Yukon, Alberta, Columbia, Hemlock, Birch, Alder, Spruce, Johnston

Cafés (numbered): 5, 51, 2, 14, 43, 13, 27, 50, 3, 22, 41, 16, 44, 46, 48, 45, 47, 18, 29, 40, 7, 10, 35, 30, 12, 49, 31, 28, 24, 39, 1, 25, 52

0   1 km

33

West Side

Vancouver's West Side is large and diverse. Fashionable neighborhoods like Shaughnessy, Kerrisdale and Point Grey sit comfortably next to such varied areas as Kitsilano, Fairview Slopes, and the University of British Columbia Endowment Lands. This variety is evident in the cafes, which embody the rich influences of the different West Side communities. Just across False Creek from Downtown, Kitsilano's coffeehouses reflect a more relaxed pace. Nearby Granville Island—a collection of renovated warehouses transformed in the 1970s into theatres, art studios, and a prosperous public market known for its fresh seafood and produce—is home to many restaurants and picturesque views. Stretching east from Granville Island is the Fairview Slopes area encompassing the beauty of False Creek up to busy Broadway. Kerrisdale, with its many fine restaurants, fashion and exclusive gift stores, is centred around 41st Avenue and East Boulevard on the way to the University of British Columbia, while South Granville and Cambie Streets cut through the West Side featuring an array of fine stores and gourmet food establishments. In all of these "neighborhoods" there are many cafes worth visiting.

West Side

Amy's Cake Shop

3396 Cambie Street
WEST SIDE
604-872-8833

Map: 3
Reference: 1
Hours: M-W 7am - 11pm,
Th - Sat 7am - 12am,
Sun 7am - 11pm
Coffee: Torrefazione Italia
Clientele: professionals, locals, and passersby
Ambience: bakery-cafe

Filled with artistic and tasty desserts, Amy's Cake Shop has a thirty-year history preparing cakes, desserts, cookies and buns for its loyal Vancouver patrons. The Mango Mousse Cake and Strawberry Mango Cheesecake are worth a drive across town. Located down the block from the Park Theatre.

Bean Around The World Coffees

4456 West 10th Avenue
POINT GREY
604-222-1400

Map: 3
Reference: 2
Hours: M-F 7am - 10pm,
Sat 7:30am - 10pm,
Sun 8:30am - 5pm
Coffee: Bean Around The World
Clientele: students, families, businesspeople
Ambience: cozy and home-style

The smell of freshly ground coffee fills the air at Bean Around The World, where you will find a wide variety of coffees, teas, cold beverages and a huge selection of grilled panini sandwiches, homemade vegetarian and non-vegetarian soups, salmon chowder, salads, samosas, wrapps, cakes and cookies. Sit by the fireplace or the window for a great view. There's also a patio deck in back.

West Side

Bean Bros.

2179 West 41st Avenue
KERRISDALE
604-266-2185

Map: 3
Reference: 3
Hours: M-F 6am - 11pm,
Sat 6:30am - 11pm,
Sun 7am - 11pm
Coffee: Bean Bros.
Clientele: families and students
Ambience: casual, friendly

A comfortable, local meeting place in the heart of Kerrisdale, Bean Bros. cafe offers fresh homemade food each day. Besides baked goods, like muffins, scones and cookies, there are sandwiches, soups and pastas for lunch and dinner. There's also a brick pizza oven. Coffee beans are freshly roasted on site.

West Side

Benny's Bagels on Broadway

2503 West Broadway
KITSILANO
604-732-9730

Map: 3
Reference: 4
Hours: M-Th 7am - 1am, F & Sat 24 hours, Sun 7am - 1am
Coffee: Bean Around The World
Clientele: artists, musicians, and students
Ambience: laid back and comfortable

Situated in the heart of Kitsilano, this is the 'original' Benny's Bagels. Adorned with unique artwork, handcrafted woodwork and steelwork, Benny's offers a variety of great coffees, teas, sandwiches, melts, cookies, cakes and waffles in its two-level complex. Bagels come in many varieties, from sesame and poppy, to cinnamon raisin and focaccia. Beer and coolers are also served.

Benny's Bagels

5728 University Boulevard
UBC
604-222-7815

Map: 3
Reference: 5
Hours: M-Sun 6:30am - 10pm
Coffee: Coloiera
Clientele: students, university instructors, staff, and residents
Ambience: friendly, cozy and inviting

A large two-level cafe at UBC's University Village, Benny's Bagels has lots of choices for hungry students, faculty, UBC hospital staff, patients, neighborhood residents and visitors. Fresh bagels made on site come in many varieties, including sesame, poppy, cinnamon raisin and focaccia. Large pretzels served with hot mustard are popular snacks on the way to, or from, class. A selection of sandwiches, melts, wrapps, lasagnas, cakes, cookies, and pastries complement the rich variety of coffees, herbal teas, and chai.

West Side

Blenz Coffee

695 West Broadway
FAIRVIEW SLOPES
604-879-2041

Map: 3
Reference: 7
Hours: M-F 6am - 11pm,
Sat 6:30am - 11pm,
Sun 6:30am - 10pm
Coffee: Blenz
Clientele: office and hospital workers, shoppers, residents, and tourists
Ambience: relaxing

At Heather and Broadway, Blenz is always busy with patrons in search of coffee and something from the vast selection of breakfast pastries, cakes, biscottis, fresh juices, sodas, and mineral water. A relaxing atmosphere, the interior features comfortable couches and window seats.

Blue Parrot Espresso Bar

2698 West 4th Avenue
KITSILANO
604-688-1173

Map: 3
Reference: 6
Hours: M-Sun 5am - 10pm
Coffee: Organic House Blend
Clientele: locals, non-locals
Ambience: comfortable, casual

All coffee, and many varieties of teas, are organic at the Blue Parrot Espresso Bar. This specialty has made the Blue Parrot well known throughout Vancouver. A selection of sandwiches and pastries is served at lunch and dinner.

West Side

Blue Parrot Espresso Bar

1689 Johnston
GRANVILLE ISLAND
604-688-5127

Map: 3
Reference: 44
Hours: M-Sun 9am - 6pm
Coffee: Organic House Blend
Clientele: locals and tourists
Ambience: scenic water view

Situated in the Granville Island Public Market overlooking False Creek, Blue Parrot offers many varieties of organic coffees and teas. Sip a beverage while watching the boats float by. A selection of sandwiches and pastries is served at lunch and dinner.

Boleto

2563 West Broadway
KITSILANO
604-739-1314

Map: 3
Reference: 8
Hours: M-Th 8am - 5pm,
F & Sat 8am - 10pm,
Sun 8am - 5pm
Coffee: Milano
Clientele: everyone by day and theatre buffs by night
Ambience: rustic elegance

Boleto is known for its European cuisine and popular organic baked breads and Artisan breads made with premium, traditional ingredients. Relax at one of this Kitsilano cafe's large wooden tables and enjoy fine pastries, such as espresso biscotti, lemon tarts and tiramisu. Intimate, candlelit dinners and an eclectic collection of wines characterize Boleto's evening menu. Gift baskets of baked delicacies are available.

West Side

Bread Garden Bakery & Cafe

1880 West 1st Avenue
KITSILANO
604-738-6684

Map: 3
Reference: 9
Hours: M-Th 6am - 11pm,
F & Sat 6am - 12am,
Sun 6am - 11pm
Coffee: JJ Bean
Clientele: people who like quick service and quality food and beverages
Ambience: cozy and comfortable

Although it began in Berkeley, California in 1973, Canada saw its first Bread Garden open at this Vancouver location in Kitsilano in 1984. Ever since, Bread Garden has delivered a consistent selection of high quality, fresh foods and beverages in a comfortable and friendly environment. The large menu includes roasted vegetable lasagna, smoked salmon quiche, noodles & cheese, "big bowls" such as the Tandoori Chicken and Spicy Asian Tofu. There are also a variety of wrapps, sandwiches, salads, and soups. Try the signature Cinnamon Knot, New York cheesecake, the mixed-berry coffeecake, carrot cake, or pear almond flan. Take home some rich croissants, French, sourdough or whole wheat breads.

West Side

Bread Garden Bakery & Cafe

2996 Granville Street
SOUTH GRANVILLE
604-736-6465

Map: 3
Reference: 49
Hours: M-Sun 24 hours
Coffee: JJ Bean
Clientele: shoppers and locals
Ambience: cozy and comfortable

Head to South Granville to satisfy your hunger at any time of day or night at this Bread Garden, open 24 hours a day.

Bread Garden Bakery & Cafe

601 West Broadway
FAIRVIEW SLOPES
604-638-0883

Map: 3
Reference: 10
Hours: M-Th 7:30am - 9pm,
F & Sat 9am - 8pm,
Sun 7:30am - 9pm
Coffee: JJ Bean
Clientele: shoppers and locals
Ambience: cozy and comfortable

See previous page for description.

West Side

Bread Garden Bakery & Cafe

2424 Main Mall
UBC
604-822-1953

Map: 3
Reference: 51
Hours: M-F 7:45am - 4pm
Coffee: JJ Bean
Clientele: students, faculty and UBC employees
Ambience: cozy and comfortable

Located inside the Forest Sciences Building on the UBC Campus. See previous page for description.

The Butler Did It

1646 West 1st Avenue
KITSILANO
604-739-3663

Map: 3
Reference: 11
Hours: M-F 7:30am - 4pm, Sat & Sun closed
Coffee: Torrefazione Italia
Clientele: surrounding businesses
Ambience: warm comfortable setting

A popular Vancouver catering company, The Butler Did It is also a great cafe near Granville Island featuring homemade hot entrees, made-to-order sandwiches, fresh salads, and soups. A wide assortment of hot and cold beverages is available. For a break during your busy day, drop by and see for yourself just how well "The Butler Did It."

West Side

Café Crepe

2861 Granville Street
SOUTH GRANVILLE
604-488-1326

Map: 3
Reference: 12
Hours: M-Th 8am - 11pm, F & Sat 8am - 12am, Sun 8am - 11pm
Coffee: Illy
Clientele: businesspeople, shoppers and tourists
Ambience: Parisian style

Dine-in or take-out from Café Crepe, a Parisian-inspired cafe known for its great food, coffee, upbeat music, and warm and inviting decor. Savory and desert crepes are prepared in front of your eyes. Ementhal Cheese & Tuna, Nutella with Banana, Maple Syrup and Lemon Sugar, are some of the most popular fillings. Specialty crepes feature your choice of liqueur and ice cream. Baguettes and panini sandwiches, which are grilled, round off the menu. Try one of the special coffees or cold drinks.

Café Madeleine

3763 West 10th Avenue
POINT GREY
604-224-5558

Map: 3
Reference: 14
Hours: M-F 11am - 8pm, Sat 9am - 9am, Sun 9am - 3pm
Coffee: House Blend
Clientele: students and professionals
Ambience: casual and relaxed

Featuring a mixture of authentic Indian and Western food, Café Madeleine emphasizes hearty breakfasts on weekends and Indian food in the evenings. The menu features 24 different breakfast items, 17 lunch choices including salads, and 13 dinner selections. Music, author readings, comedy routines, and the "Philosopher's Café," sponsored by SFU's Harbour Centre, make Café Madeleine a popular place for an entertaining and intellectually stimulating evening.

West Side

Calhoun's Bakery Cafe

3035 West Broadway
KITSILANO
604-737-7062

Map: 3
Reference: 13
Hours: M-Sun 24 hours
Coffee: Canterbury
Clientele: everyone
Ambience: funky and casual

Open 24 hours every day, Calhoun's Bakery is a popular sidewalk cafe where all of the food is homemade. Besides pastas, salads and a sandwich bar, there's ice cream and cakes. A large selection of hot and cold beverages complement your meal or quench a thirst. Students enjoy Calhoun's large wooden tables for studying.

Capers Community Market

2285 West 4th Avenue
KITSILANO
604-739-6676

Map: 3
Reference: 15
Hours: M-Sun 8am - 10pm
Coffee: Organic House Blend
Clientele: community residents
Ambience: comfortable

Adjacent to Capers natural foods market, Capers' cafe features organic and natural foods and beverages. The deli choices include soups, sandwiches, salads and baked goods. Take a seat and enjoy some breakfast, lunch, or dinner, or buy a selection to take home from one of the best natural food delis and markets on Vancouver's West Side. There is a wide selection of grocery items, magazines, and newspapers in the market.

West Side

Characters Fine Books & Coffee Bar

8419 Granville Street
WEST SIDE
604-263-4660

Map: 3
Reference: 16
Hours: M-F 7:30am - 6pm, Sat & Sun 9am - 6pm
Coffee: Salt Spring Roasting Co.
Clientele: neighborhood residents and used-book enthusiasts
Ambience: relaxed, bright and cheerful

Conveniently located inside a used bookstore, Characters Coffee Bar is the place where you can wander the stacks with a coffee or sit and converse over drinks and pastries. Featuring organic and Fair Trade coffee, Characters offers a wide assortment of muffins, scones, cookies, bagels, biscotti, homemade pies, cinnamon buns with cream-cheese icing, hot cider, milkshakes, and sundaes. Lunch items include soups, chilis and shepherds pie.

Death By Chocolate

1598 West Broadway
WEST SIDE
604-730-2462

Map: 3
Reference: 17
Hours: M-Th 7am - 12am, F 7am - 1am, Sat 12pm - 1am, Sun 12pm - 12am
Coffee: Seattle's Best Coffee
Clientele: chocolate and ice cream lovers and coffee connoisseurs
Ambience: art deco

Located on Broadway near Granville, Death By Chocolate has thirty unique dessert creations. After you place your order, watch as your selection is expertly prepared at the pastry bar. Presentation is part of the experience. Some of the most popular selections include "Split Decision," "Latin Lover," "Heaven On Earth," "Multitude Of Sins" and "French Affair." Espresso drinks, sandwiches and baked goods complement the dessert menu.

West Side

Ecco Il Pane

238 West 5th Avenue
FALSE CREEK
604-873-6888

Map: 3
Reference: 18
Hours: M-F 7:30am - 5pm, Sat 8am - 5pm, Sun closed
Coffee: Milano
Clientele: eclectic mix of neighborhood locals, tourists, and celebrities
Ambience: casual with 'Old World' charm

Like a trip to Tuscany, 'Old World' ambience fills the Ecco Il Pane bakery. Traditional Italian and Artisan breads, biscotti and dolci (Italian desserts) are baked fresh daily. Breakfasts, lunches and weekend brunches are always popular. Don't forget to take home some breads and pastries.

The Elysian Room

1778 West 5th Avenue
WEST SIDE
604-734-1778

Map: 3
Reference: 21
Hours: M-F 7am - 12am, Sat 10am - 12am, Sun 12pm - 10pm
Coffee: Organic House Blend
Clientele: locals and moviegoers
Ambience: passionate, intriguing and sophisticated

Soft, warm colours and captivating down tempo music fill the Elysian Room, located next to the Fifth Avenue Cinemas, where full meals are served for lunch and dinner besides fresh-baked muffins, scones, cookies and cakes. Before or after a movie head around the corner and enjoy something sweet and savory.

West Side

Epicurean Delicatessen

1898 West 1st Avenue
KITSILANO
604-731-5370

Map: 3
Reference: 19
Hours: M-Sat 9am - 8pm, Sun 9am - 7pm
Coffee: Epicurean blend
Clientele: professionals, computer and film industry
Ambience: warm, inviting and intimate

For a real taste of Italy, Kitsilano's Epicurean Delicatessen offers a vast assortment of homemade meals with something for everyone. The menu is filled with all kinds of pastas, veggies, meats, sandwiches, and salads that can be enjoyed at one of the indoor or outdoor tables, or packed for take-out. There is also a wide selection of Italian gelato and pastries, including custard filled croissants. The coffee is brewed from Epicurean's popular blend of beans. For an authentic Italian coffee experience, try the Epicurean Gelato, a double shot of espresso poured over a scoop of vanilla ice cream. A selection of Italian groceries, such as dry pasta, tomato sauces, antipasti, olives, olive oils and cookies are available for purchase.

Expressohead Coffee House

1945 Cornwall Avenue
KITSILANO
604-739-1069

Map: 3
Reference: 20
Hours: M-F 7:30am - 10pm, Sat & Sun 8:30am - 12am
Coffee: Café Classics
Clientele: Kitsilano residents and beach-goers
Ambience: quiet and cozy

Not far from Kitsilano Beach at the corner of Cornwall and Walnut, Expressohead is easy to find with the big cup above the entrance. It's a great place to study, read or talk, while enjoying one of the homemade sandwiches, soups, baked goods, desserts, waffles, fruit smoothies, or frappes. Local artists created the unique tables and furnishings, sculptured from wood and metal.

West Side

Fish Cafe

2053 West 41st Avenue
KERRISDALE
604-267-3474

Map: 3
Reference: 22
Hours: T-Sun 11:30am - 3pm, Mon - Sun 5pm - 9pm
Coffee: Torrefazione Italia
Clientele: fresh seafood enthusiasts, locals
Ambience: casual, warm, inviting

If you like great fish and seafood, whether grilled, blackened or deep fried, Fish Cafe is the place to go. This Kerrisdale eatery serves great meals with your choice of rice or fries. Salads are also on the menu. Popular items include prawn curry, big seafood platter, and fresh halibut with your choice of tarter, lemon or garlic butter sauces.

Granville Island Coffee House

16 - 1551 Johnston
GRANVILLE ISLAND
604-682-7865

Map: 3
Reference: 45
Hours: M-Th 8:30am - 6:30pm, F & Sat 8:30am - 8pm, Sun 8:30am - 6:30pm
Coffee: Café Classics
Clientele: False Creek area residents, tourists
Ambience: warm, cozy, relaxing

At the Public Market, tucked away behind the Arts Club Theatre on the waterfront, Granville Island Coffee House offers a quiet respite for weary shoppers who want a brief escape from Island crowds and noise. Besides coffee, there is plenty of ice cream, soup, bagels, sandwiches and lunch specials. The outdoor seating provides a peaceful and relaxing time with a view of the boats and water. Internet access available.

West Side

Higher Grounds

2300 West Broadway
KITSILANO
604-733-0201

Map: 3
Reference: 23
Hours: M-F 6:30am - 10pm, Sat 7:30am - 10pm, Sun 7:30am - 9pm
Coffee: House Blend
Clientele: neighborhood
Ambience: inviting and friendly

Higher Grounds is situated within a Kitsilano heritage building featuring big bright windows, comfortable seating and beautiful art displays. Drop in and enjoy a sandwich, soup, salad, pastries or other desserts. Don't forget the coffee!

Java Hut Espresso Co.

797 West 16th Avenue
FAIRVIEW
604-873-6388

Map: 3
Reference: 24
Hours: M-F 6am - 10pm, Sat 6:30am - 10pm, Sun 7am - 10pm
Coffee: JJ Bean
Clientele: locals and hospital employees
Ambience: Caribbean decor and cozy

This bustling neighborhood cafe is popular among area residents and nearby hospital workers. A variety of hot and cold lunch and dessert items, including cheesecake, fruit pies, and muffins, are on the menu at this upbeat and friendly place known for its Caribbean atmosphere.

West Side

JJ Bean House of Coffee

GRANVILLE ISLAND
604-685-0613

Map: 3
Reference: 46
Hours: M-Sun 7:30am - 6pm
Coffee: JJ Bean
Clientele: locals and tourists
Ambience: Warm, wood-with-copper highlights, take-away only cafe

Located in the hustle and bustle of the Granville Island public market, JJ Bean House of Coffee serves its own brand. The company roasts it, blends it, and serves it in a variety of appetizing forms. If you want food visit the market, but if you want a hot beverage join the line! This site only sells 'liquid assets.'

Kino Café

3456 Cambie Street
WEST SIDE
604-875-1998

Map: 3
Reference: 25
Hours: M-F 3pm - 1am, Sat & Sun 11am - 1am
Coffee: Ionia
Clientele: entertainment seekers
Ambience: old-European cafe, warm and candlelit atmosphere

If you enjoy music, the Kino Café, located next to the Park Theatre, is the place to be in the evening. There's live Gypsy-Swing on Mondays, Jazz on Tuesdays, and the ever-popular Flamenco nights from Wednesdays through Sundays. Enjoy pastas, tapas, chicken parmagiana, cakes and ice cream. Beverages include sangria, Guinness beer-on-tap, lattes and cappuccinos.

West Side

La Petite France

2655 Arbutus Street
KITSILANO
604-734-7844

Map: 3
Reference: 26
Hours: T-F 8am - 7pm, Sat & Sun 8am - 6pm
Coffee: Illy
Clientele: neighborhood residents & French community
Ambience: friendly, warm

La Petite France's specialty is the preparation of homemade exquisite and delicious French and Viennese pastries. Besides the fine selection of sweets, there are many specialties, including foie gras, duck confit and pates. Drop by this popular Kitsilano bakery and cafe for some pastries to take home, or stay a while and indulge yourself on some European treats. A popular dessert is the "Patete," a French pastry that is meant to resemble a potato but is a delicate custard-filled sponge cake topped with marzipan and dusted with cocoa.

La Solace Café

4883 Mackenzie Street
WEST SIDE
604-266-4029

Map: 3
Reference: 27
Hours: M-F 7am - 7pm, Sat 8:30am - 7pm, Sun 10am - 4pm
Coffee: Torrefazione Italia
Clientele: neighborhood
Ambience: cozy, warm and unique

Located just north of Kerrisdale, La Solace Cafe serves a variety of espresso beverages along with homemade soups, salads and grilled focaccia sandwiches. Your children are welcome to play with toys and read their favorite books while you enjoy a coffee and a bite to eat.

West Side

Max's Bakery & Delicatessen

3105 Oak Street
FAIRVIEW
604-733-4838

Map: 3
Reference: 28
Hours: M-Sun 6:30am - 11pm
Coffee: JJ Bean
Clientele: everyone
Ambience: neighborhood deli

Max's Bakery & Delicatessen serves a rich variety of international foods with something for everyone at its three busy West Side locations. From knishes and samosas to salmon Wellington and turkey sandwiches, the selections are homemade and available all day, everyday. There is a wide assortment of baked goods, breakfast items, breads, fine pastries and cakes.

Max's Bakery & Delicatessen

521 West 8th Avenue
FAIRVIEW
604-873-6297

Map: 3
Reference: 29
Hours: M-F 6:30am - 6pm, Sat 7:30am - 5:30pm, Sun 10am - 4pm
Coffee: JJ Bean
Clientele: everyone
Ambience: neighborhood deli

See above for description.

West Side

Max's Bakery & Delicatessen

1488 West 11th Avenue
SOUTH GRANVILLE
604-736-8830

Map: 3
Reference: 30
Hours: M-F 7:30am - 11pm, Sat 8:30am - 11pm, Sun 8:30am - 9pm
Coffee: JJ Bean
Clientele: everyone
Ambience: neighborhood deli

See previous description.

Meinhardt Fine Foods

3002 Granville Street
SOUTH GRANVILLE
604-732-4405

Map: 3
Reference: 31
Hours: M-Sat 8am - 9pm, Sun 9am - 9pm
Coffee: Illy
Clientele: eclectic mix of area residents
Ambience: bright and open

At Meinhardt Fine Foods, have a seat and enjoy some lunch and dinner items or place an order to go. There is an extensive selection of homemade muffins, scones, granola, chicken pies, soups, salads, and made-to-order sandwiches. There's also a large daily assortment of hot and cold dishes. The grocery store is filled with gourmet favourites from all over the world, featuring imported items from France, England and Italy. Besides the food, there are cookbooks, newspapers and flowers.

West Side

Mum's Gelati

2028 Vine Street
KITSILANO
604-738-6867

Map: 3
Reference: 32
Hours: M-Sat 7:30am - 12am, Sun 8am - 12am
Coffee: Coliera
Clientele: locals
Ambience: rustic

Located just off 4th Avenue, Mum's Gelati serves homemade Italian ice cream and freshly baked goods. The mocha chip gelato and spumoni are popular choices. There are also a variety of fruit-flavoured gelati. Try one of the picturesque lattes or cappuccinos.

The Naam

2724 West 4th Avenue
KITSILANO
604-738-7151

Map: 3
Reference: 33
Hours: M-Sun 24 hours
Coffee: Organic House Blend
Clientele: vegetarians, students, and night owls
Ambience: earthy

The Naam is a very busy full-service vegetarian restaurant in the heart of Kitsilano. In winter the burning fireplace keeps patrons warm while summertime lounging in the beautiful garden patio is a popular diversion for many. Live music every evening. Blues, folk and jazz are the styles which add to the Naam's unique atmosphere. For big appetites, try the Farmer's Breakfast, Huevos Rancheros, Scrambled Tofu, or a giant fresh fruit crepe. There are muffins, scones, granola and porridge for lighter fare. Lunch and dinner favourites include the sesame fries with miso gravy, enchiladas, burritos, vegi-burger platters, and unique "Dragon bowls" with rice and sauces.

West Side

Panne Rizo Bakery Café

1939 Cornwall Avenue
KITSILANO
604-736-0885

Map: 3
Reference: 34
Hours: T-F 10am - 6pm, Sat 9:30am - 5:30pm
Coffee: Illy
Clientele: wheat free, food allergies and Celiac crowd
Ambience: warm and welcoming

Those with allergies will be very happy to know that all products at Panne Rizo are totally wheat and gluten free (most are lactose free as well). Everything at Panne Rizo is made from scratch each day. There are lots of food choices available, from grilled paninis, lasagna, and chicken potpie, to breads, buns, focaccia, pizzolas, muffins, and cinnamon buns. Don't forget the cookies, brownies, and Danishes, all of which are wheat free but with the taste and texture of fine wheat baking. The European-style cafe serves a variety of coffees to go along with its baked goods.

Seattle's Best Coffee

2706 Granville Street
SOUTH GRANVILLE
604-734-2706

Map: 3
Reference: 35
Hours: M-F 6am - 10pm, Sat 6:30am - 11pm, Sun 7am - 7pm
Coffee: Seattle's Best Coffee
Clientele: residents and south Granville shoppers
Ambience: a temporary oasis

Located on South Granville near the Stanley Theatre, Seattle's Best Coffee serves freshly brewed coffee selections. The coffee beans are custom-roasted at the company's plant in Seattle. The "Post Alley" coffee blend is a popular choice. For an extra jolt, add a second shot of espresso to any of the espresso-based beverages for no additional cost. The chai latte is a delicious alternative for tea drinkers. To complement the beverages, there's a selection of freshly baked goods, including cookies and muffins.

West Side

Solly's Bagelry

2873 West Broadway
KITSILANO
604-738-2121

Map: 3
Reference: 36
Hours: M-Th 8am - 6pm, F 7am - 7pm, Sat 8am - 7pm, Sun 8am - 6pm
Coffee: Seattle's Best Coffee
Clientele: everyone
Ambience: warm and inviting

Solly's Bagelry is a neighborhood bakery and deli that offers the best in traditional homemade Jewish cooking and baking. This West Side location opened a few years ago. There is a great selection of soups and sandwiches for dine-in or take-out. Have a seat inside or outside and enjoy a bagel. There are many different kinds from which to choose, and there's also a different variety of bagel offered each month, such as Pumpkin in October and Chocolate Chip in February. Popular items include the 'famous' cinnamon buns, chocolate 'babka' (sweet dough with chocolate inside), and onion 'biallies' (like a mini pizza without the cheese or sauce).

Sophie's Cosmic Cafe

2095 West 4th Avenue
KITSILANO
604-732-6810

Map: 3
Reference: 37
Hours: M-Th 8am - 9:30pm, F & Sat 9am - 10pm, Sun 8am - 9pm
Coffee: House Blend
Clientele: local residents, university students
Ambience: happy, eclectic, and comfortable

Don't be surprised if you see a line up of people waiting to get into Sophie's Cosmic Cafe, where the interior decoration is one of the things that make this cafe so unique. Inside you'll be reminded of a vintage '60's rec room. Breakfast items include waffles, pancakes, and egg dishes. Lunch and dinner feature a variety of entrees from chicken burgers to soup. Try an espresso milkshake for a cool coffee alternative to a basic brew.

West Side

Starbucks

3492 Cambie Street
WEST SIDE
604-872-3911

Map: 3
Reference: 52
Hours: M-Sat 6am - 11pm, Sun 7am - 10:30pm
Coffee: Starbucks
Clientele: local residents
Ambience: comfortable

Located near the Park Theatre, this busy cafe offers all of Starbucks' coffee and tea blends. Try the ever-popular "Caffe Latte," steamed milk with a rich shot of espresso, topped with foamed milk, or the "Frappuccino," a creamy, low-fat blend of coffee and milk, customized with mocha, espresso, caramel or syrups. Food selection includes sandwiches, baked goods and desserts.

Starbucks

1500 West 2nd Avenue
GRANVILLE ISLAND
604-736-5477

Map: 3
Reference: 47
Hours: M-Th 5:30am - 10pm, F - Sun 6am - 10:30pm
Coffee: Starbucks
Clientele: businesspeople and students
Ambience: comfortable and upbeat

Located at the entrance of Granville Island, this two-level cafe with outdoor patio offers all of Starbucks' coffee and tea blends. Try the "Frappuccino," a creamy, low-fat blend of coffee and milk, customized with mocha, espresso, caramel or syrups. The "Latte Macchiato" contains steamed milk topped with foam and marked with a ristretto shot ("short pull") poured through the centre of the drink. Food selection includes sandwiches, baked goods and desserts.

West Side

Terra Breads

2380 West 4th Avenue
KITSILANO
604-736-1838

Map: 3
Reference: 38
Hours: M-Sat 7am - 6pm, Sun 7am - 5:30pm
Coffee: JJ Bean
Clientele: neighborhood locals and food lovers
Ambience: bright and warm

At Terra Breads in Kitsilano you can enjoy your breakfast or lunch while watching the bakers in the background shaping breads and pulling fresh baked goods out of the oven. An Artisan bakery and cafe, Terra Breads is a perfect place to read the morning paper while enjoying cinnamon buns, cookies, sandwiches or soups. Popular items include the poppy or sesame seed challah, the ginger cookies, and the Potato-Rosemary Focaccia bread, which is only available on Sundays, Wednesdays, and Thursdays.

Terra Breads

1689 Johnston Street
GRANVILLE ISLAND
604-685-3102

Map: 3
Reference: 48
Hours: M-Sun 9am - 6pm
Coffee: JJ Bean
Clientele: locals, tourists, and students
Ambience: public market

At Terra Breads in the Public Market you can watch the bakers in the background shaping breads and pulling fresh baked goods out of the oven. Enjoy the cinnamon buns, and cookies. Popular items include poppy and sesame seed challah (braided egg bread), olive rolls, pumpkinseed bread, ginger cookies, and Belgian chocolate brownies.

West Side

Tomato Fresh Food Café

3305 Cambie Street
WEST SIDE
604-874-6020

Map: 3
Reference: 39
Hours: M-Sun 9am - 10pm
Coffee: House Blend
Clientele: film/TV industry, musicians, artists, and businesspeople
Ambience: bistro, casual elegance, comfortable

On the corner of 17th and Cambie, literally wrapped around a barbershop, you will find a unique city bistro. Tomato Fresh Food Cafe has a wide selection of appetizers, soups, salads, sandwiches, and dessert items, as well as a juice bar and wine list. "Urbanly hip, intelligent, healthy cooking" is Tomato's motto. Entrees range from a polenta-stuffed portobello with roasted garlic tomato sauce and spinach spatzle, and grilled salmon on brazed leaks, to the Moroccan-spiced lamb with vegetable couscous, and chicken marinated in garlic and oregano with mashed potatoes and roasted green beans.

Tony's Coffee

111 - 805 West Broadway
FAIRVIEW SLOPES
604-871-0007

Map: 3
Reference: 40
Hours: M-F 6am - 7:30pm, Sat 8am - 4:30pm
Coffee: Tony's
Clientele: businesspeople, medical professionals, and hospital staff
Ambience: relaxing and comfortable

Lively jazz music fills Tony's Coffee, a popular and busy cafe located near Vancouver General Hospital. There's a great selection of baked goods, sandwiches, soups, salads, and a pleasant outdoor patio.

West Side

Torrefazione Italia

2154 West 41st Avenue
KERRISDALE
604-267-1003

Map: 3
Reference: 41
Hours: M-F 6am - 10pm, Sat 7am - 10pm, Sun 8am - 8pm
Coffee: Torrefazione Italia
Clientele: locals
Ambience: "Warmth of Italy"

Seattle-based Torrefazione Italia provides Vancouver with an elegant Italian atmosphere in which to enjoy a latte or cappuccino. Each month a different artist's paintings are showcased. There is a great selection of Italian sandwiches, pastries, and gelati. The coffee beans come from Torrefazione's own roasting plant in Seattle. Live music is featured Friday evenings.

Truffles Bistro

1943 Cornwall Avenue
KITSILANO
604-733-0162

Map: 3
Reference: 42
Hours: M-Th 5pm - 1am, F 5pm - 2am, Sat 12pm - 2am, Sun 12pm - 12am
Coffee: House Blend
Clientele: students, Kits residents
Ambience: European eclectic

Close to the Burrard Street Bridge and the H.R. MacMillan Space Centre in Kitsilano, Truffles Bistro specializes in homemade European dishes including beef lasagna, vegetable cannelloni, foccacia bread, yam and sweet potato soup, and chocolate truffles. Music adds to the ambience.

West Side

Yoka's Coffee & Honey

3171 West Broadway
KITSILANO
604-738-0905

Map: 3
Reference: 43
Hours: M-F 9am - 6pm,
Sat 9am - 5:30pm,
Sun 10am - 5pm
Coffee: Yoka's
Clientele: neighborhood and citywide
Ambience: old-fashioned "country-style"

One of the oldest coffee roasters in Vancouver, Yoka's roasts its own beans to maintain quality and ensure freshness. European furnishings and 1930's vintage roaster add to the ambience. Coffee beans are available for purchase by the pound. Enjoy some espresso or tea.

Late-Night Cafes

What if it happens to be midnight and you can't sleep or you're about to start your night shift? Why not drop by one of the following cafes for a place to enjoy some late night food and drink. Hours vary. Some are open until 1 or 2 am while others are open 24 hours a day. Check the index in the back for locations and neighborhood maps.

Calhoun's Bakery Cafe - 3035 West Broadway
Neighborhood: KITSILANO
Coffee: Canterbury
Open 24 hours

Kino Café - 3456 Cambie Street
Neighborhood: WEST SIDE
Coffee: Ionia
Open until 1am

The Grind & Gallery - 4124 Main Street
Neighborhood: MAIN
Coffee: Canterbury
Open 24 hours

Montmartre - 4362 Main Street
Neighborhood: MAIN
Coffee: House Blend
Open until 2am on weekends

The Naam - 2724 West 4th Avenue
Neighborhood: KITSILANO
Coffee: House Blend
Open 24 hours

Truffles Bistro - 1943 Cornwall Avenue
Neighborhood: KITSILANO
Coffee: House Blend
Open until 2am on weekends

Map 4
East Side

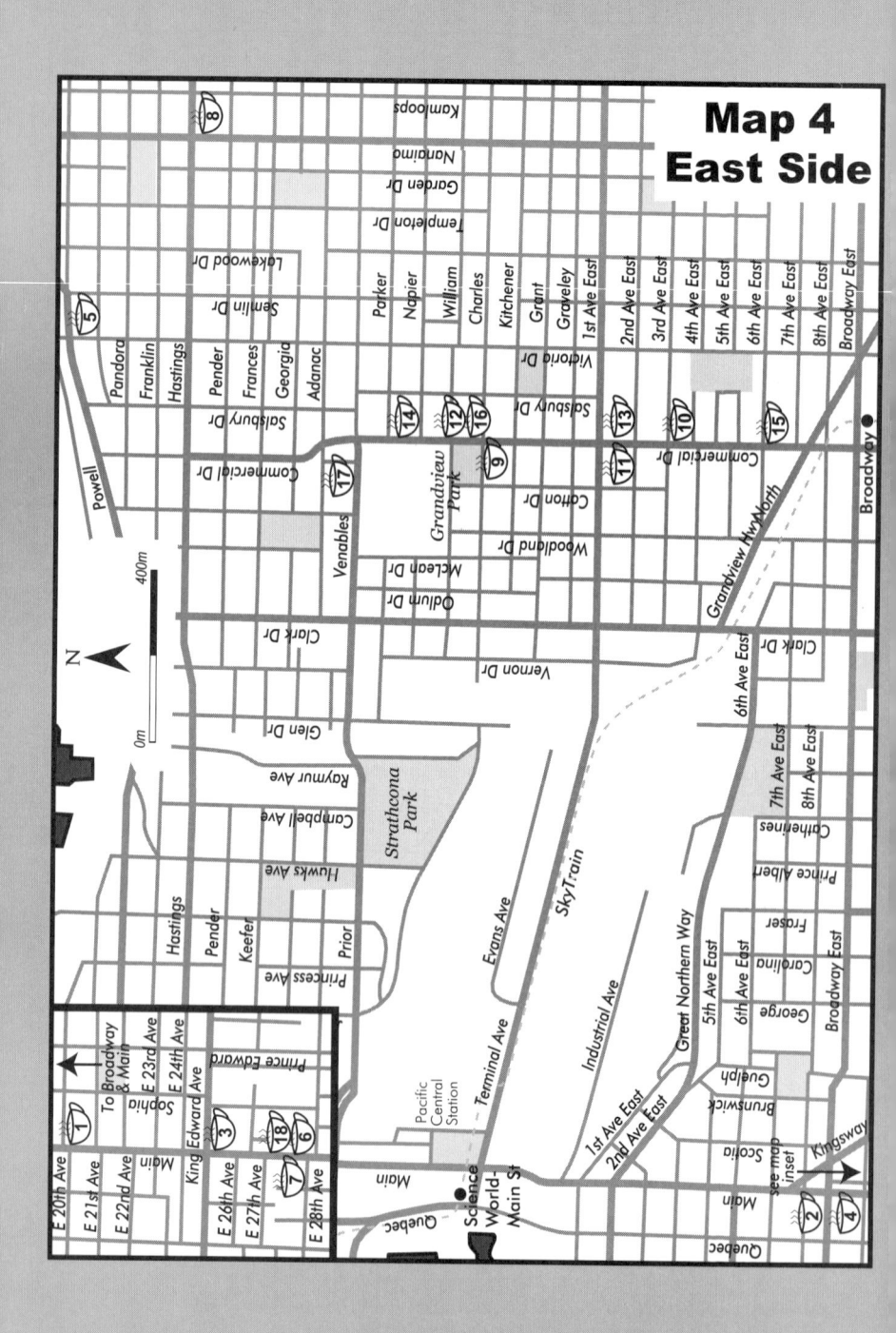

East Side

From Main Street to Boundary Road, Vancouver's East Side is just as diverse as Vancouver's West Side. Spanning a vast area from Cambie to Clark Drive and 16th Avenue down to 1st Avenue, the historic Mount Pleasant neighborhood is a mecca for artists. Main Street, between 33rd and 16th Avenues, is a blend of ethnic restaurants, antique shops and vintage clothing stores. Commercial Drive, still fondly referred to as "Little Italy" due to the historic Italian presence, is home to many different national influences, including Italian, Spanish, Portuguese, Cuban, and Greek. Not only do stores, restaurants, and bakeries shaped by these cultures make "The Drive" a popular destination for locals throughout the Lower Mainland, but each of these "neighborhoods" attract visitors who want to broaden their cultural horizons. Experience some "East Side" diversity at the following cafes.

East Side

Abbruzzo Cappuccino Bar

1321 Commercial Drive
COMMERCIAL
604-254-2641

Map: 4
Reference: 9
Hours: M-Sun 7am - 1am
Coffee: House Blend
Clientele: families, sports fans
Ambience: casual

Abbruzzo Cappuccino Bar's big screen TV draws people from all over town to watch sports events. Coffee is another reason. Besides the hot and cold beverages, there is homemade Italian-style pizza, baked sausages with pepper in foccacia, and cold cut sandwiches.

Artistico Greek Cafe

1938 Commercial Drive
COMMERCIAL
604-251-2511

Map: 4
Reference: 10
Hours: M-Th 11am - 11pm, F - Sun, 11am - 12am
Coffee: House Blend
Clientele: locals
Ambience: cozy, casual and comfortable

At Artistico have a seat on a couch or at one of the large tables and enjoy live Greek music and classical harp. Located in a heritage building with lots of windows, couches and plants, traditional Greek food is served at Artistico. The menu features such favourites as souvlaki and gyros, spanakopitas (spinach pie), tiropita (cheese pie), roast lamb, and a selection of vegetarian items. There are many coffee selections to accompany the Greek desserts, including baklava, bougatsa, and galactobouriko.

East Side

Anona Fine Foods

3610 Main Street
MAIN
604-255-2932

Map: 4
Reference: 1
Hours: M-Sun 10am - 3pm
Coffee: JJ Bean
Clientele: locals and loyal clientele from all over town
Ambience: relaxed and warm

This Main Street cafe features a variety of savory items, such as knishes and latkes (potato pancakes), as well as sweets and baked goods. Try the ginger cookies or chocolate cherry brownies. Everything is homemade. There is also a good selection of vegetarian and vegan items. Anona is also a catering company and provides food for weddings, bar/bat mitzvahs and office lunches. Art exhibitions featuring local artists change frequently.

Caffe Calabria

1745 Commercial Drive
COMMERCIAL
604-253-7017

Map: 4
Reference: 11
Hours: M-Th 7am - 11pm, F & Sat 7am - 12am, Sun 7am - 11pm
Coffee: Calabria Special Blend
Clientele: everyone
Ambience: a touch of Italy

Among the oldest Italian coffee bars in Vancouver, at Caffe Calabria you will be treated like one of the many celebrities that have visited over the years. Their pictures adorn the walls. Adding to the authentic Italian atmosphere, Frank, the owner, loves to serenade customers with operatic arias. Calabria serves its own blend of coffee. Enjoy a cappuccino or another espresso beverage with something from the vast selection of Italian pastries, cookies and cakes. The Italian menu includes big foccacia sandwiches, ice cream, and biscotti.

67

East Side

Cuppa Joe Coffee Co.

189 East Broadway
MOUNT PLEASANT
604-709-4123

Map: 4
Reference: 2
Hours: M-Sun 6am - 10pm
Coffee: Cuppa Joe
Clientele: "from all walks of life"
Ambience: fun, friendly and urban

Located in the historic Lee Building constructed in 1912, Cuppa Joe is an urban coffee bar that is serious about producing a perfect cup of coffee. An extensive line is carried including certified organic and Fair Trade coffees. There are also chai lattes, fruit-tea freezes, iced coffee drinks, wrapps, and baked goods. Cuppa Joe is a roaster and supplies coffee beans to other coffee bars, cafes, delis, grocery stores, offices and organic home delivery companies.

The Grind & Gallery

4124 Main Street
MAIN
604-874-1588

Map: 4
Reference: 3
Hours: M-Sun 24 hours
Coffee: Canterbury
Clientele: students, locals, and night owls
Ambience: cozy and casual

Open 24 hours a day, The Grind is busy all the time! A cafe within a gallery that showcases the work of artists, the Grind has plenty of large wooden tables in the front and back areas. Baked goods complement the list of espresso-based beverages.

East Side

Havana

1212 Commercial Drive
COMMERCIAL
604-253-9119

Map: 4
Reference: 12
Hours: M-Th 11am - 12am, F 11am - 1am, Sat 10am - 1am, Sun 10am - 12am
Coffee: Café Classic
Clientele: cross section
Ambience: "Old Cuban"

Fashioned after Havana's La Bodeguita Del Medio, the famous Cuban meeting place of poets and intellectuals, where the likes of Hemingway spent much of their time, Vancouver's 'Havana' is a popular restaurant and art gallery. Offering 'Nuevo Latino Cuisine' in a casual setting, Havana has an all-weather patio that overlooks Grandview Park and the city skyline. The menu includes La Santa Maria (chicken/rice dish), Caribbean Fried Chicken, and Trinidadian Curry. A 60-seat theatre in the back showcases a wide variety of performances, from local productions, poetry readings, dancing (including dance instruction), to jazz and cinema.

Lugz Coffee Lounge

2525 Main Street
MOUNT PLEASANT
604-873-6766

Map: 4
Reference: 4
Hours: M-F 6:30am - 11:30pm, Sat 7:30am - 11:30pm, Sun 9am - 11pm
Coffee: Berardo
Clientele: locals, artists, musicians, and office workers
Ambience: casual

Located in Mount Pleasant, Lugz Coffee Lounge makes espresso with Berardo beans, imported from Rome, Italy. Besides the large selection of coffee drinks, there are juices, smoothies, teas, and beverages made with soymilk. Sandwiches and pastries are available. Another popular feature is Internet access to check your e-mail or surf the web.

East Side

JJ Bean House of Coffee

1904 Powell Street
EAST SIDE
604-254-0161

Map: 4
Reference: 5
Hours: M-F 6:30am - 4pm, Sat 9am - 4pm, Sun closed
Coffee: JJ Bean
Clientele: "The Commercial Drive hippie, the West Side preppy, the North Shore mom, the wide-eyed suburban commuter, the downtown suit and the East Side dweller."
Ambience: Buzz of a real live roaster in its noisy, smoky, aroma laden atmosphere

John Neate Jr. and his crack squad of coffee purists started JJ Bean in 1996. So why not try a coffee at its source? JJ Bean still roasts all of its beans on site. Complement your coffee with one of the muffins. But once out of the oven, they're usually all gone before they've had a chance to cool. Cranberry is among the most popular.

Montmartre

4362 Main Street
MAIN
604-879-8111

Map: 4
Reference: 6
Hours: M-W 4pm - 1am, Th 11am - 1am, F & Sat 11am - 2am, Sun 11am - 1am
Coffee: House Blend
Clientele: varied
Ambience: Parisian

Ever wanted to experience a little bit of Paris without leaving Vancouver? Just as the original Montmartre Quarter in Paris was once a mecca for artists, writers and poets, Vancouver's Montmartre on Main Street is a place you'll be entertained with live performances of flamenco, jazz, cabaret and folk music, as well as poetry readings. Intimate and casual, Montmartre features French savory and sweet crepes, and North African foods.

East Side

Solly's Bagelry

189 East 28th Avenue
MAIN
604-872-1821

Map: 4
Reference: 7
Hours: T-Sat 7am - 7pm, Sun 8am - 6pm
Coffee: Seattle's Best Coffee
Clientele: everyone
Ambience: warm and inviting

People come from all over town to pick-up their supply of bagels. Popular varieties include onion, poppy, sesame, cinnamon raisin, and whole wheat. There are also the famous cinnamon buns, chocolate babkas, knishes, and rugelagh. There's also poppy, sesame and plain challah. Every month the art changes on the walls... but you must be a kid to participate! Children create all the artwork at Solly's. There is a great selection of soups and sandwiches for dining in or takeout. All the food is homemade at this East Side neighborhood bakery/deli offering some of the best in traditional Jewish baking.

Starbucks

1752 Commercial Drive
COMMERCIAL
604-251-5397

Map: 4
Reference: 13
Hours: M-F 6am - 9pm, Sat 6:30am - 9pm, Sun 7am - 9pm
Coffee: Starbucks
Clientele: local residents
Ambience: comfortable

Located at 2nd Avenue and Commercial, this cafe offers all of Starbucks' coffee and tea blends. Enjoy the "Caffe Latte," steamed milk with a rich shot of espresso, topped with foamed milk, or the "Frappuccino," a creamy, low-fat blend of coffee and milk, customized with mocha, espresso, caramel or syrups. Food selection includes sandwiches, baked goods and desserts.

East Side

Starry Dynamo Café

4342 Main Street
MAIN
604-875-9975

Map: 4
Reference: 18
Hours: M-Sun 9:30am - 12:30am
Coffee: House Blend
Clientele: talented, creative
Ambience: unpretentious, unique

Alive and spirited, the Starry Dynamo Cafe is a self-described "public living room," entirely unpretentious and unique, where customers contribute to the atmosphere with philosophical battles and creative discussions. There are live musical performances, literary, spoken word and 'open stage' events. Internet access is also available. Try one of the many sandwiches and soups, with a wide selection for vegetarians, vegans and non-vegetarians. There are also plenty of desserts, coffees, teas and chai.

Sweet Tooth Cafe

2404 East Hastings Street
EAST SIDE
604-255-6997

Map: 4
Reference: 8
Hours: M-F 6am - 8pm, Sat 8am - 8pm, Sun 8am - 7pm
Coffee: Torrefazione Italia
Clientele: shoppers, residents, office workers, eclectic mix
Ambience: cozy and friendly

Neighborhood regulars drop in for their homemade food and pastry featuring a variety of favourites such as freshly baked scones, muffins, cheesecake, and pies, as well as soups and chili. Thai food is the specialty of the house. Sweet Tooth Cafe is equally popular among kids and seniors.

East Side

Tony's Deli

1046 Commercial Drive
COMMERCIAL
604-253-7422

Map: 4
Reference: 14
Hours: M-F 7:30am - 5:30pm, Sat & Sun closed
Coffee: Torrefazione Italia
Clientele: "those who love panini"
Ambience: comfortable, casual

Tony's Deli is famous for its huge menu of hot and cold paninis. Popular varieties include the "Athena Fresca" with fresh spinach, artichoke hearts, feta cheese, sun-dried and fresh tomatoes, and the "West Coast Salmon" with smoked salmon, spinach, cream cheese, Spanish onions, capers with a hint of lemon zest. The "Turkey Trattoria" has fresh turkey breast, sun-dried tomatoes, Swiss cheese, lettuce and herbs. There are also salads and desserts to complement the coffees. Office and event catering is available.

Torrefazione Coloiera

2206 Commercial Drive
COMMERCIAL
604-254-3723

Map: 4
Reference: 15
Hours: M-F 7:30am - 5pm, Sat 9am - 5pm, Sun closed
Coffee: JJ Bean
Clientele: 'new age hippies' and locals
Ambience: relaxed

Visit this newly renovated cafe for an authentic Italian coffee. The atmosphere is warm and friendly, but visitors take their coffee very seriously here, so experience some flavour and variety.

East Side

Turk's Coffee House

1276 Commercial Drive
COMMERCIAL
604-255-5805

Map: 4
Reference: 16
Hours: M-Th 7am - 11:30pm, F & Sat 7:30m - 12am, Sun 8am - 11:30pm
Coffee: Milano
Clientele: artists, professionals, moms, and children
Ambience: comfortable, artistic

At Turk's enjoy some hot coffee in a cool atmosphere. There are lots of food choices available, from cinnamon buns, brownies, loafs, dessert squares, to such savory items as spicy black bean wrapps, vegi pot pies and samosas. Try one of the unique drinks, such as the "Turkachino," iced coffee blended with ice, milk, vanilla, espresso, and whipped cream. Turk's also has an art gallery with exhibits that change frequently.

Uprising Breads Bakery

1697 Venables Street
COMMERCIAL
604-254-5635

Map: 4
Reference: 17
Hours: M-F 7am - 7pm, Sat & Sun 7am - 6pm
Coffee: Casa Del Caffe
Clientele: locals, commuters
Ambience: lively

An East Side landmark for over 25 years, Uprising Breads bakes all of its whole grain breads, buns, muffins, scones, and cookies on the premises. Popular items include lemon poppy seed muffins, blueberry cornmeal muffins, white chocolate cherry scones, and ginger snap cookies. There's a large selection of homemade sandwiches everyday, but get there early or your favourite may be long gone.

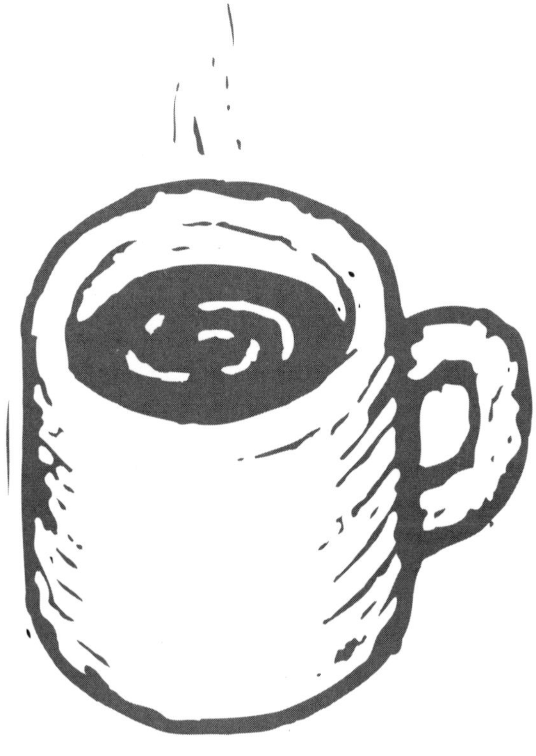

Internet Cafes

If you'd like to check your e-mail or you just want to browse the Web, why not have a beverage and a snack at the same time? The following cafes offer Internet access for their patrons. Rates for Internet access vary from one cafe to another. Some offer free access with purchase of food or beverage while others charge by the minute or hour. So, if you need to surf the Internet, why not drop by a cafe and enjoy the amenities. Check the index in the back for locations and neighborhood maps.

Lingo Cyber Bistro

547 Seymour Street, Vancouver, Phone: 604-331-9345

Coffee: Torrefazione Italia
Hours: M-F 7am - 7pm, Sat 8am - 4pm
Computers: PC's
Cost: $2.85 for 15 minutes; $4.00 for 30 minutes, $6.85 per hour
Special offers: With food purchase of $7 (min), receive 15 minutes of Internet access for free.

Lugz Coffee Lounge

2525 Main Street, Vancouver, Phone: 604-873-6766

Coffee: Berardo
Hours: M-F 6:30am -11:30pm, Sat 7:30am - 11:30pm, Sun 9am - 11pm
Computers: PC
Cost: $2.00 per 15 minutes or $7 per hour

Granville Island Coffee House

16 - 1551 Johnston, Vancouver, Phone: 604-682-7865

Coffee: Café Classics
Hours: M-Th 8:30am - 6:30pm, F & Sat 8:30am - 8pm, Sun 8:30am - 6:30pm
Computers: PC
Cost: With any purchase, the first 30 minutes are free, then $1.00 for each15 minute increment thereafter.

Internet Cafes

Starry Dynamo Café
4523 Hastings Street, Burnaby, Phone: 604-320-0999

Coffee: House Blend
Hours: M-Sun 9:30am - 12:30am
Computers: PC
Cost: $1.00 for 15 minutes; $2.00 for 30 minutes; $4.00 per hour
Special offers: With any purchase, receive 15 minutes of Internet access for free.

Jitters Coffee House
4342 Main Street, Vancouver, 604-875-9975

Coffee: Arbuckles
Hours: M-Th 8am - 11pm, F & Sat 8am - 12am, Sun 1pm - 6pm
Computers: PC
Cost: $1.50 for 15 minutes; $3.00 for 30 minutes; $6.00 per hour

Map 5
West Vancouver & North Vancouver

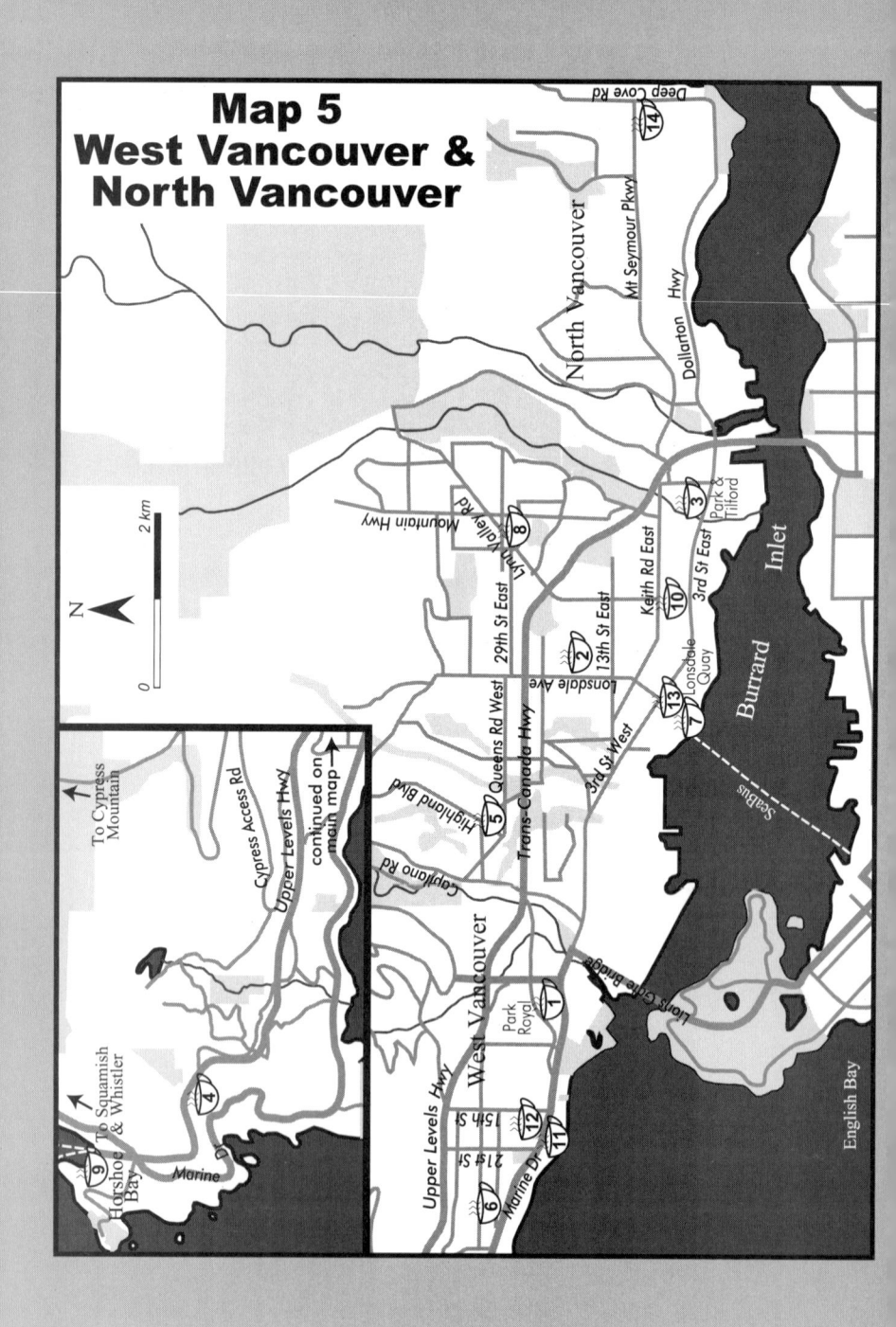

West Vancouver

A short commute across Lion's Gate Bridge from downtown Vancouver, West Vancouver is a picturesque district of residential neighborhoods, sea walks and beaches bounded east to west by the Capilano River and Howe Sound, and north to south by the North Shore mountains and Burrard Inlet. West along Marine Drive is scenic Ambleside and Dundarave, with their exclusive boutiques and restaurants. Further northwest is Horseshoe Bay on Howe Sound where BC Ferries leave everyday for places on Vancouver Island, Bowen Island, and the Sunshine Coast. Each of these areas offers West Vancouver tourists and locals many attractive destinations, where cafes provide a refreshing stop along the way.

West Vancouver

Bread Garden Bakery & Cafe

550 Park Royal North
WEST VAN
604-925-0181

Map: 5
Reference: 1
Hours: M-Th 6am - 12am,
F & Sat 6am - 1am,
Sun 6am - 12am
Coffee: JJ Bean
Clientele: shoppers, moviegoers, and area residents
Ambience: cozy and comfortable

At Park Royal Mall on the north side of Marine Drive, Bread Garden offers a large selection of high quality fresh foods and beverages. The menu includes roasted vegetable lasagna, smoked salmon quiche, Thai Chicken Wrapp, California Sushi Wrapp, and "big bowls," such as the Curry Masala and Red Lentil Dahl. There are also a variety of sandwiches, salads, and soups. Try the signature Cinnamon Knot, mango cheesecake, or chocolate macadamia pecan pie.

Cove Fine Foods

5775 Marine Drive
WEST VAN
604-913-2471

Map: 5
Reference: 4
Hours: M-Th 8am - 6pm,
Fri & Sat 8am - 9pm,
Sun 8am - 6pm
Coffee: House Blend
Clientele: locals and boaters
Ambience: casual elegance

Located in a wooden building with a copper roof across from the marina, Cove Fine Foods serves coffee made from beans it imports from Chiapas, Mexico. Custom-created sandwiches, salads, soups, and ice cream are on the menu. There's also a wide selection of prepared foods, including skewers, marinated meats, cheeses, and homemade salad dressings to enjoy on site, at home, or, given the ideal surroundings, on a boat.

West Vancouver

Delany's in Dundarave

2424 Marine Drive
DUNDARAVE
604-921-4466

Map: 5
Reference: 6
Hours: M-Sun 6am - 10pm
Coffee: JJ Bean
Clientele: area residents
Ambience: "old style" classic coffeehouse

At Delany's in the Dundarave area, experience many varieties of coffees while enjoying a 2nd shot of espresso at no extra charge. To satisfy your hunger, there are plenty of muffins, scones, cinnamon buns, cookies, biscotti, brownies, pies, cakes and sandwiches, including a daily special, all freshly made.

The Lookout Coffee House

6409 Bay Street
HORSESHOE BAY
604-921-9205

Map: 5
Reference: 9
Hours: M-Sun 8:30am - 4:30pm
Coffee: Kicking Horse Coffee
Clientele: tourists, North Shore locals, and urban dwellers
Ambience: historical, peaceful, bright

For a scenic view of Horseshoe Bay and the waterfront, visit the "Lookout." Housed in a custom-built structure with high ceilings, big bright windows, and outdoor patio with large umbrellas, the Lookout offers lattes, cappuccinos, and cool beverages with a broad selection of scones, pies, cinnamon buns and cookies, all from the Savary Island bakery. Don't overlook the fresh fruit juices and "fruit juice slushy," a refreshing alternative on a warm day. Of particular interest to tourists is a glass-covered, wooden table map that identifies BC attractions. There are also plenty of tourist brochures to sites throughout the province. On Sunday mornings enjoy live musical performances featuring flute, Celtic harp and violin.

West Vancouver

Savary Island Pie Company

1533 Marine Drive
AMBLESIDE
604-926-4021

Map: 5
Reference: 12
Hours: M-Sat 5am - 10pm, Sun 5am - 6pm
Coffee: Yoka's
Clientele: West Van residents
Ambience: comfortable

Centrally located on Marine Drive in West Vancouver, Savary Island Pie Company is well known for its pies and baked goods. Other food items include omelettes, pot pies, grilled-cheese sandwiches, the Vegi sandwich and the "French," with ham, tomatoes, cheese, mustard, mayo and butter. As you'd expect, there is a wide assortment of pies available, including raspberry, blueberry, rhubarb, and lemon buttermilk. Live music, poetry and author readings are featured regularly.

Torrefazione Italia

1860 Marine Drive
AMBLESIDE
604-913-6781

Map: 5
Reference: 11
Hours: M-F 6am - 10pm, Sat 7am - 10pm, Sun 8am - 8pm
Coffee: Torrefazione Italia
Clientele: area residents, office workers
Ambience: Italian warmth

Seattle-based Torrefazione Italia provides West Vancouver with an elegant Italian atmosphere in which to enjoy a latte or cappuccino. Each month a different artist's paintings are showcased. There is a great selection of Italian sandwiches and pastries. The coffee beans come from Torrefazione's own roasting plant in Seattle. Live music is featured every Thursday evening.

North Vancouver

Across Lion's Gate Bridge from downtown Vancouver is North Vancouver, a large commercial and residential centre on the North Shore just east of the Capilano River at the foot of the Lower Mainland's two most visited mountains, Grouse and Seymour. The Second Narrows Bridge is another way to reach this bustling suburb. At the south end of Lonsdale Avenue, which is North Vancouver's main north-south thoroughfare and shopping area, is Lonsdale Quay, a busy and scenic public market with plenty of stores and restaurants. Access BC Transit's SeaBus there. These catamaran passenger ferries provide commuters a popular water link between the North Shore and downtown Vancouver. Northwest of Lonsdale is Edgemont Village, a wooded slope below Grouse Mountain that maintains its traditional appeal as an alpine village with unique boutiques and shops. East of Lonsdale is the Park & Tilford Shopping Centre, close to Highway 1 and the Second Narrows Bridge. Lynn Valley Road is a major route that heads northeast past Lynn Canyon Centre to Lynn Canyon Park. Further east is Deep Cove, which overlooks the waterway of Indian Arm on its eastern flank, and the municipality of Burnaby across the water to the south. Throughout this region are cafes that will please outdoor adventurers on their way to mountain escapes, and locals who just want a place in their neighborhood to visit and enjoy some refreshments.

North Vancouver

Bread Garden Bakery & Cafe

116 East 17th Street
LONSDALE
604-904-1182

Map: 5
Reference: 2
Hours: M-Sun 6am - 11pm
Coffee: JJ Bean
Clientele: locals
Ambience: cozy and comfortable

A large selection of high quality fresh foods and beverages is available at North Vancouver's two Bread Gardens. The menu includes roasted vegetable lasagna, smoked salmon quiche, and "big bowls," such as the Curry Masala and Red Lentil Dahl. There is a variety of sandwiches, salads, and soups. Desserts include the Cinnamon Knot, carrot cake, and pear almond flan.

Bread Garden Bakery & Cafe

360 - 333 Brooksbank Avenue
PARK & TILFORD
604-983-8483

Map: 5
Reference: 3
Hours: M-F 6am - 11pm, Sat & Sun 8am - 12am
Coffee: JJ Bean
Clientele: locals
Ambience: cozy and comfortable

See above for description.

North Vancouver

Delany's In The Village

3099 Edgemont Boulevard
EDGEMONT VILLAGE
604-985-3385

Map: 5
Reference: 5
Hours: M-Sun 6am - 11pm
Coffee: JJ Bean
Clientele: village residents
Ambience: "old style" classic coffeehouse

At Delany's in the heart of Edgemont Village enjoy a coffee with a "second shot" of espresso at no extra charge. To satisfy your hunger, there are, plenty of muffins, scones, cinnamon buns, cookies, biscotti, brownies, pies, cakes and sandwiches, including a daily special, all freshly made.

Garibaldi's Espresso

102 - 123 Carrie Cates Court
LONSDALE QUAY
604-986-9228

Map: 5
Reference: 7
Hours: M-Sun 9:30am - 6:30pm
Coffee: House Blend
Clientele: shoppers, commuters, and office workers
Ambience: family environment

Located in the Lonsdale Quay market, Garibaldi's Espresso offers grilled paninis, toasted and cold sandwiches, salads, lasagna, "all-day" breakfasts, pastries, and cold Italian sodas. There's also a big screen TV. Enjoy!

North Vancouver

Indigo Books Café

1221 Lynn Valley Road
LYNN VALLEY
604-904-7970

Map: 5
Reference: 8
Hours: M-Th 9am - 10pm, F & Sat 9am - 11pm, Sun 10am - 8pm
Coffee: Olympic
Clientele: book lovers, information and entertainment seekers
Ambience: New York "beat" cafe

Located inside the Indigo Books and Music Store in Lynn Valley Centre, the Indigo Café provides an excellent opportunity to read some excellent literature while indulging in specialty coffees and decadent desserts. There is a wide selection of hot and cold sandwiches and pastries.

Mount Royal Bagel Factory

701 Queensbury Avenue
LONSDALE
604-904-1116

Map: 5
Reference: 10
Hours: M-Sat 7am - 6pm, Sun 8am - 4pm
Coffee: Reingold
Clientele: bagel lovers, commuters from all over
Ambience: bagel factory

Have some freshly brewed coffee while enjoying a bagel at the Mount Royal Bagel Factory. Hand-rolled and boiled to perfection, popular bagel varieties include poppy, sesame, onion, and cinnamon (plain or whole-wheat dough). Besides being known throughout the Lower Mainland for its great bagels, Mount Royal also has the distinction of being the first 'certified' kosher bagelry in BC. All of the coffee drinks are made with organic Reingold coffee.

North Vancouver

Starbucks

131 Esplanade Avenue
LONSDALE QUAY
604-986-3797

Map: 5
Reference: 13
Hours: M-F 6am - 10pm, Sat & Sun 7am - 9pm
Coffee: Starbucks
Clientele: businesspeople and tourists
Ambience: comfortable and upbeat

You'll find all of Starbucks' coffee and tea blends in North Vancouver. These are just two of the popular sites. Try the "Caffe Latte," steamed milk with a rich shot of espresso, topped with foamed milk, or the "Frappuccino," a creamy, low-fat blend of coffee and milk, customized with mocha, espresso, caramel or syrups. The "Latte Macchiato" contains steamed milk topped with foam and marked with a ristretto shot ("short pull") poured through the centre of the drink. Food choices include sandwiches, baked goods and desserts.

Starbucks

391 North Dollarton Highway
DEEP COVE
604-929-5962

Map: 5
Reference: 14
Hours: M-W 6am - 9pm, Th & F 6am - 10pm, Sat 6:30 - 10pm, Sun 7am - 10pm
Coffee: Starbucks
Clientele: local residents
Ambience: casual, warm, inviting

Breakfast Cafes

On weekends—and weekdays if your schedule allows—there's nothing better than starting your day with a great breakfast, some good coffee, and a newspaper at a local cafe. While many cafes offer breakfast items on their menus, others make it a priority. The following is a list of some of the better known cafes offering extensive breakfast choices—some available all day long! Check the index in the back for locations and neighborhood maps.

Benny's Bagels
2503 West Broadway, Vancouver, Phone: 604-732-9730

Bojangles on the Waterfront
1506 Coal Harbour Way, Vancouver, Phone: 604-687-6599

Cafe Amore
4502 Dawson Street, Burnaby, Phone: 604-298-3135

Caffe Artigiano
1101 West Pender Street, Vancouver, Phone: 604-685-5333

Café Crepe
1032 Robson Street, Vancouver, Phone: 604-448-0045

Café Madeleine
3763 West 10th Avenue, Vancouver, Phone: 604-224-5558

Canadian Maple Delights
769 Hornby Street, Vancouver, Phone: 604 682-6175

Breakfast Cafes

Chef Bernard's Café
1 - 4573 Chateau Boulevard, Whistler, Phone: 604-932-7051

Garibaldi's Espresso
2724 West Fourth Avenue, Vancouver, Phone: 604-738-7151

Moonpennies
103-1112 West Pender Street, Vancouver, Phone: 604-669-6092

The Naam
2724 West Fourth Avenue, Vancouver, Phone: 604-738-7151

Savary Island Pie Company
1533 Marine Drive , West Vancouver, Phone: 604-926-4021

Solly's Bagelry
189 East 28th Avenue, Vancouver, Phone: 604-872-1821
2873 West Broadway, Vancouver, 604-738-2121

Sophie's Cosmic Cafe
2095 West Fourth Avenue, Vancouver, Phone: 604-732-6810

Tomato Fresh Food Cafe
3305 Cambie Street, Vancouver, Phone: 604-874-6020

Wendel's Books & Cafe
103-9233 Glover Road, Fort Langley Phone: 604-513-2238

Map 6
Richmond & Delta

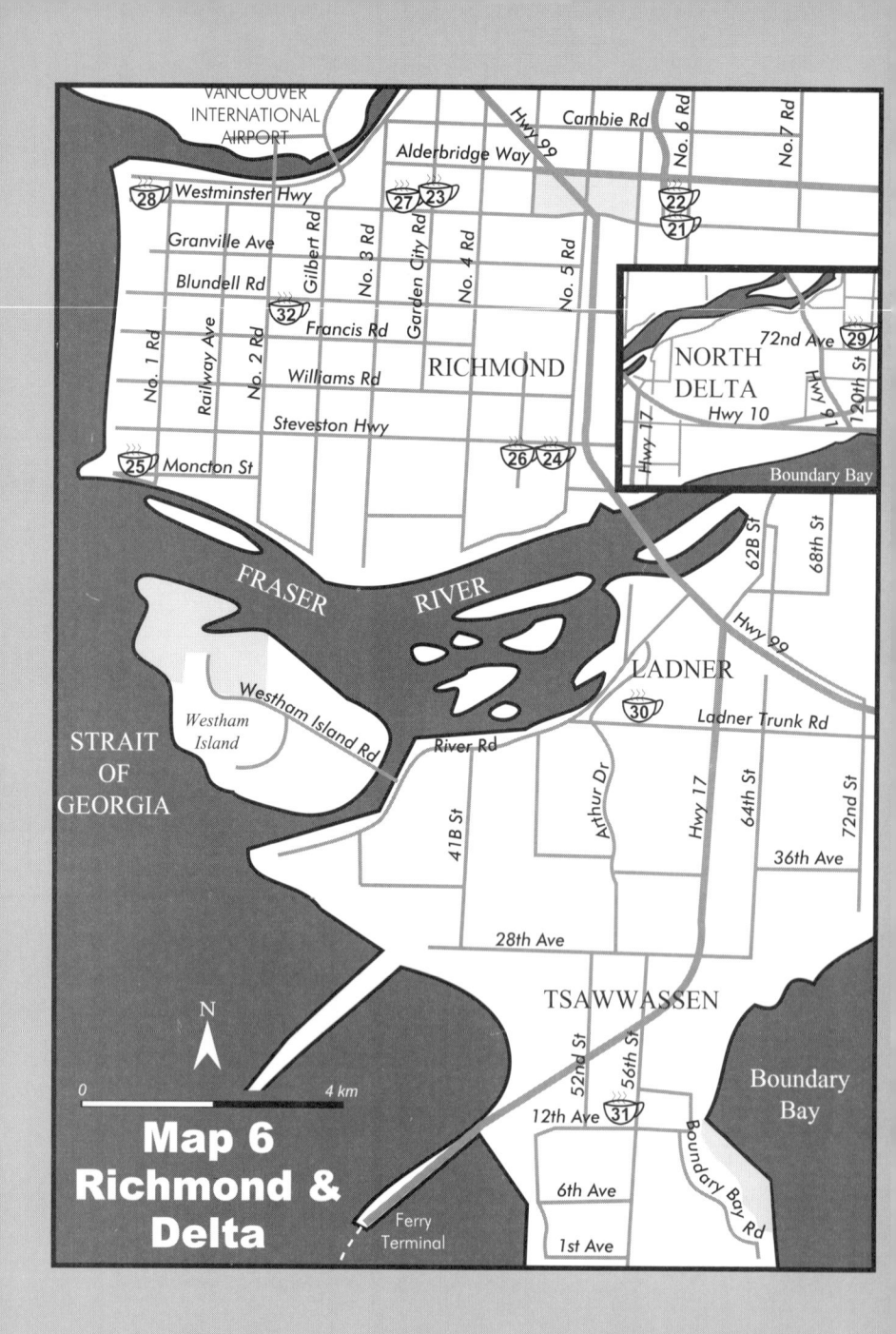

Richmond

Encircled by the North Arm and South Arm of the Fraser River, with Georgia Strait flanking the west, the city of Richmond is a growing urban and rural setting known for its blend of large shopping malls, farms, and sprawling residential communities. Though connected by bridges to Vancouver on the north and by tunnel to Delta in the south, Richmond is well worth the time to explore since there are plenty of "neighborhoods" with cafes to satisfy the food and beverage cravings of visitors and residents alike. The busy high-tech community of Crestwood can be found at No. 6 Road just north of Westminster Highway. To the west is Landsdowne, Richmond's central shopping district at No. 3 Road. The residential area of Terra Nova is further west at No. 1 Road, north of Westminster Highway. The historic community of Steveston, famous for its fishing village and water views, occupies the vast area of Richmond's southern parts along the Fraser.

Richmond

Brass & Beans

1118 - 13351 Commerce Parkway
CRESTWOOD
604-214-8620

Map: 6
Reference: 21
Hours: M-F 6:30am - 3pm, Sat & Sun closed
Coffee: Crown
Clientele: "high-tech techies," computer workers
Ambience: warm atmosphere

In a business park surrounded by high-tech companies, Brass & Beans has become the place to go for out-of-office meetings and daily escapes. There's a great selection of breakfast items along with popular lunch specials, including a chicken sandwich made with Brass & Beans' homemade bread.

Bread Garden Bakery & Cafe

120 - 13711 International Place
CRESTWOOD
604-248-0191

Map: 6
Reference: 22
Hours: M-F 7am - 7pm, closed Sat & Sun
Coffee: JJ Bean
Clientele: High-tech crowd
Ambience: cozy and comfortable

Bread Garden has three popular sites in Richmond with an extensive selection of high quality fresh foods and beverages. The menu features roasted vegetable lasagna, smoked salmon quiche, noodles & cheese, and "big bowls," such as the Curry Masala and Red Lentil Dahl. There are also a variety of wrapps, sandwiches, salads, and soups. Try the signature Cinnamon Knot, mango cheesecake, or chocolate macadamia pecan pie.

Richmond

Bread Garden Bakery & Cafe

8380 Lansdowne Road
LANSDOWNE
604-273-5888

Map: 6
Reference: 23
Hours: M-Th 6am - 1am,
F & Sat 6am - 2am,
Sun 6am - 1am
Coffee: JJ Bean
Clientele: local shoppers
Ambience: cozy and comfortable

Bread Garden Bakery & Cafe

1020 - 11660 Steveston Highway
STEVESTON
604-271-5642

Map: 6
Reference: 24
Hours: M-F 6am - 11pm, Sat & Sun 7am - 11pm
Coffee: JJ Bean
Clientele: shoppers, locals, and tourists
Ambience: cozy and comfortable

Richmond

Craving On Bay

210 - 37921 Bayview Street
STEVESTON
604-275-3753

Map: 6
Reference: 25
Hours: M-Th 9am - 8pm, Fri 9am - 9pm, Sat 8am - 9pm, Sun 9am - 5pm
Coffee: Crown
Clientele: area residents, seniors, and tourists
Ambience: casual, cozy

Located in the village of Steveston, Craving on Bay is the place to go to enjoy a meal or a snack. The menu is full of diverse offerings, from soups, chicken caesar salad, feta salad, baked salmon, halibut fish & chips to turkey burgers, Spanish chicken wrapp, and pasta entrees, such as the "Creamavera Penne" or the "Mexicasa Pasta." There are also many vegetarian selections. Beverages include "Chai latte," "Mexican Hot Chocolate" and the "Spanish Coffee."

Death By Chocolate

11688 Steveston Highway
STEVESTON
604-274-2462

Map: 6
Reference: 26
Hours: M-F 8am - 12am, Sat 10am - 1am, Sun 11am - 12am
Coffee: Seattle's Best Coffee
Clientele: chocolate and ice cream lovers and coffee connoisseurs
Ambience: art deco

At the corner of Steveston Highway and No. 5 Road is Death By Chocolate, where the presentation is definitely part of the experience! Watch expert pastry chefs create one of the thirty unique 'custom-designed' dessert creations. A few of the most popular include "Between The Sheets," "Latin Lover," "Ebony & Ivory," "Multitude Of Sins" and "Crumble In My Arms." There is a long list of sandwiches and baked goods, such as muffins, cookies, and dessert bars, and many espresso drinks from which to choose.

Richmond

Starbucks

8100 No. 2 Road
RICHMOND
604-241-7842

Map: 6
Reference: 32
Hours: M-F 5:30am - 11pm,
Sat 6am - 11pm,
& Sun 6am - 10:00pm
Coffee: Starbucks
Clientele: businesspeople and locals
Ambience: comfortable and upbeat

You'll find all of Starbucks' coffee and tea blends in Richmond. Try the "Caffe Latte," steamed milk with a rich shot of espresso, topped with foamed milk, or the "Frappuccino," a creamy, low-fat blend of coffee and milk, customized with mocha, espresso, caramel or syrups. The "Latte Macchiato" contains steamed milk topped with foam and marked with a ristretto shot ("short pull") poured through the centre of the drink. Food selections include sandwiches, baked goods and desserts.

Starbucks

8111 Acroyd Road
LANDSDOWNE
604-279-9676

Map: 6
Reference: 27
Hours: M-F 5:30am - 11pm,
Sat 6am - 11pm,
& Sun 6am - 10:00pm
Coffee: Starbucks
Clientele: locals, shoppers and businesspeople
Ambience: comfortable and upbeat

Richmond

Starbucks

100 - 3677 Westminster Highway
TERRA NOVA
604-207-1177

Map: 6
Reference: 28
Hours: M-F 6am - 11pm,
Sat 6:30am - 11pm,
& Sun 7am - 11:00pm
Coffee: Starbucks
Clientele: locals
Ambience: comfortable

See previous entry for description.

Delta

With farming and fishing the historic mainstays of the region, Delta retains much of its rural charm in an increasingly urban environment. The South Arm of the Fraser River to the north, the Georgia Strait to the west, Boundary Bay to the south, and the city of Surrey to the east border the Corporation of Delta. Today the municipality is divided into the three distinct communities of North Delta, Ladner, and Tsawwassen. While residential neighborhoods occupy much of North Delta, farms are the main features of Ladner. Tsawwassen, known for its beautiful beaches and good windsurfing, leads to the BC Ferries that transport cars, bicyclists and their occupants to Vancouver Island, the Gulf Islands and up the Inside Passage to Port Hardy and Prince Rupert. So, on route to the Tsawwassen Ferry Terminal or on your commute to work, why not pick up a coffee or tea along the way.

Delta

Starbucks

7221 120th Street
NORTH DELTA
604-543-9797

Map: 6
Reference: 29
Hours: M-F 6am - 10pm, Sat & Sun 6:30am - 10pm
Coffee: Starbucks
Clientele: locals
Ambience: relaxing

For all of Starbucks' trademark coffee and tea blends in Delta, come to these cafes! Among the most popular are the "Caffe Mocha," a mix of mocha syrup and espresso with steamed milk, topped off with whipped cream, and the "Cappuccino," the classic European-inspired beverage that contains a shot of espresso blended with steamed milk, capped off with a layer of creamy foam. Try the baked goods and desserts.

Starbucks

5263 Ladner Trunk Road
LADNER
604-940-8394

Map: 6
Reference: 30
Hours: M-F 5am - 10:30pm, Sat & Sun 5:30am - 7:30pm
Coffee: Starbucks
Clientele: locals
Ambience: comfortable

Delta

Starbucks

1 - 1359 56th Street
TSAWWASSEN
604-943-9668

Map: 6
Reference: 31
Hours: M-F 5:30am - 10pm,
Sat & Sun 6am - 10pm
Coffee: Starbucks
Clientele: locals and tourists
Ambience: busy

Chai Tea Cafes

From Russia to India, chai (which rhymes with "pie") is the word for tea. Although there are many regional variants, Indian chai has become the beverage of choice at many cafes in North American cities in recent years. Vancouver is no exception to this trend! Made with rich black tea, heavy milk, sweetener, and spices, from cardamom, cinnamon, to ginger, Indian chai is appreciated for its soothing effect. The cafes below feature extensive chai menus from chai latte, chai milkshakes, chocolate chai, non-fat chai, to decaffeinated chai. Try some and you'll likely find it hard to resist a second cup!

Benny's Bagels
2503 West Broadway
KITSILANO

Bojangles Café
785 Denman Street
WEST END

Cuppa Joe
189 East Broadway
MOUNT PLEASANT

Grab-a-Java
Unit 2 - 33093 7th Avenue
MISSION

The Lookout Coffee House
6409 Bay Street
HORSESHOE BAY

Chai Tea Cafes

Mario's Coffee Express
595 Howe Street
DOWNTOWN

Seattle's Best Coffee
1137 Hamilton Street
YALETOWN

Wendel's Books & Café
103 - 9233 Glover Road
FORT LANGLEY

Map 7
Burnaby

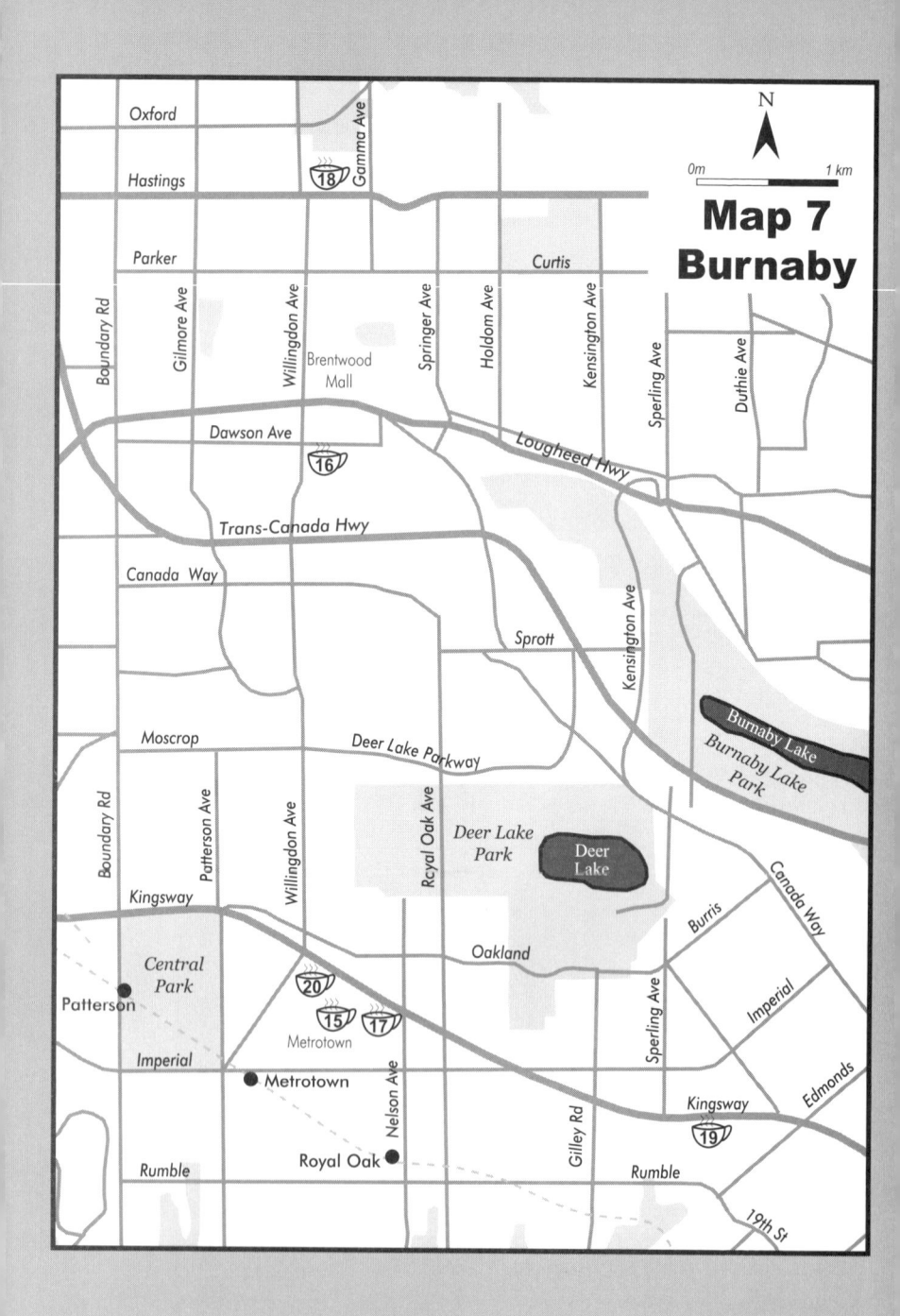

Burnaby

Located in the middle of the Lower Mainland region, the city of Burnaby occupies a diverse mix of residential, commercial and recreational areas between the cities of Vancouver to the west, and Port Moody, Coquitlam and New Westminster to the east. Burrard Inlet and the North Arm of the Fraser River form Burnaby's north and southern frontiers. Within these boundaries are many points of interest, including Simon Fraser University atop Burnaby Mountain, BC Institute of Technology on Willingdon Avenue, and "neighborhoods" positioned around busy commercial areas. North Burnaby along Hastings Street features specialty shops and restaurants. Brentwood Mall on Lougheed Highway just off Willingdon attracts local shoppers and students from nearby BCIT. Further south is Metrotown, BC's largest shopping centre with over 500 businesses, conveniently accessible by the SkyTrain. Not far from Burnaby's Deer Lake Park is Middlegate, around the always-busy Kingsway thoroughfare. In all of these areas are cafes that should satisfy the diverse tastes of local shoppers, students, and visitors.

Burnaby

Bread Garden Bakery & Cafe

4575 Central Boulevard
METROTOWN
604-435-5177

Map: 7
Reference: 15
Hours: M-Th 6:30am - 12am, F & Sat 6:30am - 1am, Sun 6:30am - 12am
Coffee: JJ Bean
Clientele: shoppers, and locals
Ambience: cozy and comfortable

Located on the south side of Metrotown, Bread Garden offers a wide choice of high quality fresh foods and beverages. The menu includes roasted vegetable lasagna, smoked salmon quiche, noodles & cheese, and "big bowls," such as the Curry Masala and Red Lentil Dahl. There are also a variety of wrapps, sandwiches, salads, and soups. Try the signature Cinnamon Knot, mango cheesecake, or chocolate macadamia pecan pie.

Cafe Amore

4502 Dawson Street
BRENTWOOD
604-298-3135

Map: 7
Reference: 16
Hours: M-F 7am - 5pm, Sat & Sun closed
Coffee: Ionia
Clientele: business and trades people
Ambience: warm, casual, comfortable decor

At this family-owned cafe close to Brentwood Mall, enjoy homemade foods from breakfast items, grilled panini sandwiches and burgers to pizza, pastas, salads, soups, and desserts. At Cafe Amore, there are many espresso beverages from which to choose, including cappuccinos and lattes. All are made from one of the most popular Italian roasted coffee brands, Ionia. Cafe Amore also caters.

Burnaby

Death By Chocolate

4883 Kingsway
METROTOWN
604-436-2462

Map: 7
Reference: 17
Hours: M-Th 8am - 11pm, F & Sat 8am - 1am, Sun 11am - 11pm
Coffee: Seattle's Best Coffee
Clientele: chocolate and ice cream lovers and coffee connoisseurs
Ambience: art deco

At the corner of Kingsway and Nelson, experience the presentation and the flavour at Death By Chocolate! Watch expert pastry chefs create one of the thirty unique 'custom-designed' dessert creations. A few of the most popular include "Between The Sheets," "Latin Lover," "Ebony & Ivory," "Multitude Of Sins" and "Crumble In My Arms." There is a long list of sandwiches and baked goods, such as muffins, cookies, and dessert bars, and many espresso drinks from which to choose.

Jitters Coffee House

4523 Hastings Street
NORTH BURNABY
604-320-0999

Map: 7
Reference: 18
Hours: M-Th 8am - 11pm, F & Sat 8am - 12am, Sun 1pm - 6pm
Coffee: Arbuckles
Clientele: locals, students, businesspeople, and music fans
Ambience: cozy meeting place

At Jitters Coffee House, you'll be entertained with live music on Thursday, Friday and Saturday evenings. The walls of the cafe are decorated with art, which changes monthly. Surf the net at high speed while enjoying a selection of delicious homemade wrapps, pies, soups, salads, cinnamon buns, cookies, and breakfast items. Hot and cold beverages include Italian sodas, smoothies, and frappe drinks. So, why not "Drop your hat and stay awhile." It's Jitters' motto!

Burnaby

Myles Of Beans Coffee House

7010 Kingsway
MIDDLEGATE
604-524-3700

Map: 7
Reference: 19
Hours: M-Th 8am - 10pm, F 8am - 11pm, Sat 9am - 11pm, Sun 11am - 10pm
Coffee: JJ Bean
Clientele: businesspeople and locals
Ambience: relaxed, casual

On Kingsway in Burnaby's Middlegate neighborhood, Myles of Beans offers a variety of vegetarian foods, along with cookies, muffins, desserts, and sandwiches. For your entertainment, live music is featured nightly. There are also poetry evenings.

Starbucks @ Chapters

1174 - 4700 Kingsway
METROTOWN
604-431-9996

Map: 7
Reference: 20
Hours: M-Sun 9am - 11pm
Coffee: Starbucks
Clientele: businesspeople and shoppers
Ambience: comfortable and upbeat

Located inside Metrotown Eaton Centre's huge Chapters bookstore, you'll find all of Starbucks' coffee and tea blends plus a lot of great books! Try the "Caffe Latte," steamed milk with a rich shot of espresso, topped with foamed milk, or the "Frappuccino," a creamy, low-fat blend of coffee and milk, customized with mocha, espresso, caramel or syrups. The "Latte Macchiato" contains steamed milk topped with foam and marked with a ristretto shot ("short pull") poured through the centre of the drink. Enjoy some baked goods and desserts.

Business-Meeting Cafes

Looking for a place to meet business associates outside of the workplace? These are just a few of the many cafes near neighborhood business districts that provide an atmosphere conducive to "working away from the office." Check the index in the back for locations and neighborhood maps.

Brass & Beans
1118 - 13351 Commerce Parkway, Richmond
Neighborhood: CRESTWOOD

Café Amore
4502 Dawson Street, Burnaby
Neighborhood: BRENTWOOD

Café Artigiano
1101 West Pender Street, Vancouver
Neighborhood: FINANCIAL DISTRICT

Starbucks
700 West Pender Street, Vancouver
Neighborhood: DOWNTOWN

The Butler Did It
1646 West 1st Avenue, Vancouver
Neighborhood: KITSILANO

Map 8
Coquitlam

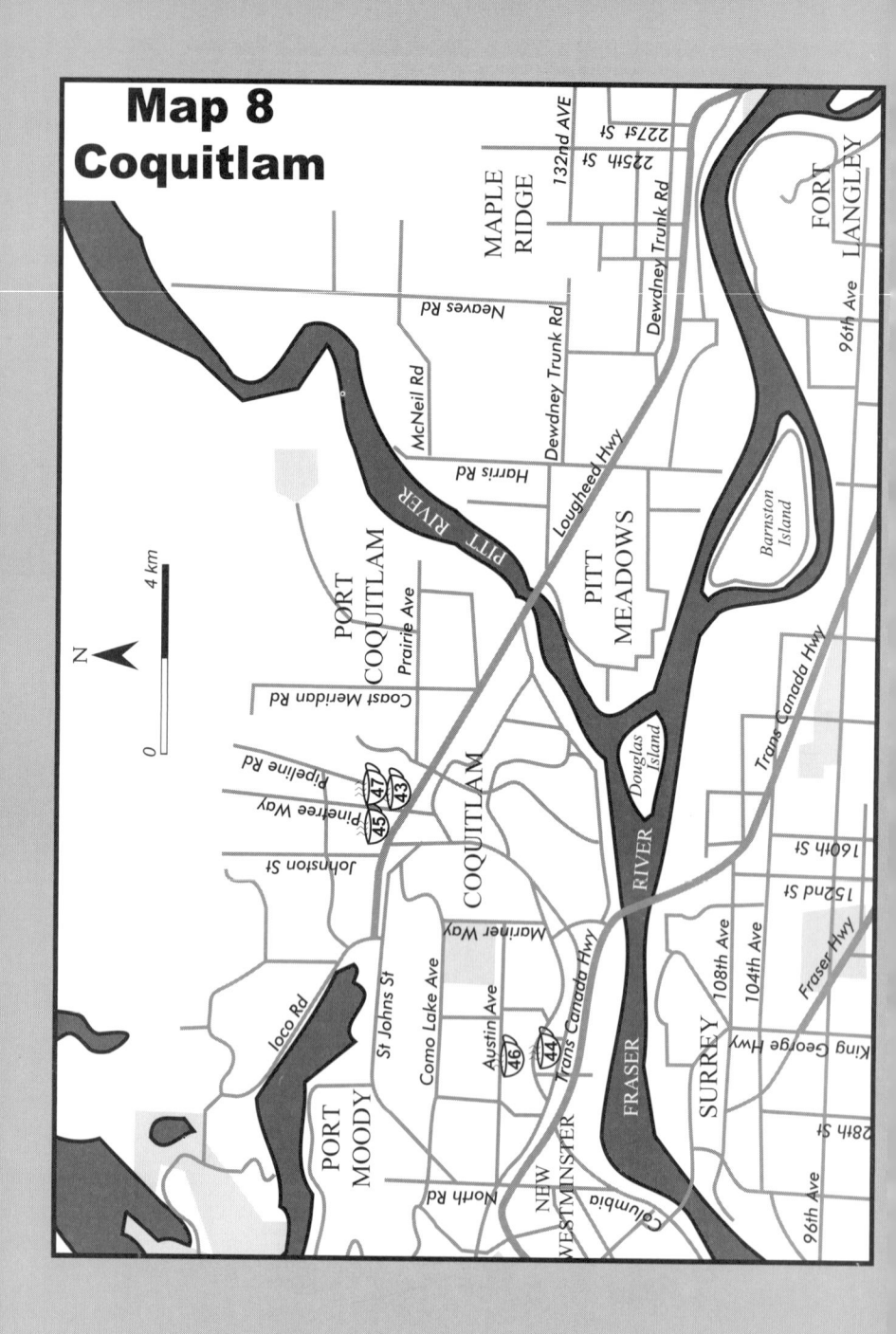

Coquitlam

The growing city of Coquitlam, bordered by Burrard Inlet and Port Moody to the north, the Fraser River to the south, and Burnaby to the west, is a thriving residential, industrial and commercial area in Vancouver's Lower Mainland. You'll find cafes in many neighborhoods including Pinetree in the Town Centre area near Lougheed Highway, and Schoolhouse in west Coquitlam, extending across to Austin Heights. Grab a coffee before starting your morning commute.

Coquitlam

Bread Garden Bakery & Cafe

15 Pinetree Shopping Centre
2991 Lougheed Highway
PINETREE 604-945-9494

Map: 8
Reference: 43
Hours: M-Th 6am - 11pm,
F & Sat 6am - 12am,
Sun 6am - 11pm
Coffee: JJ Bean
Clientele: local shoppers
Ambience: cozy and comfortable

The two popular Bread Garden locations in Coquitlam have an extensive selection of high quality fresh foods and beverages. The menu features roasted vegetable lasagna, smoked salmon quiche, noodles & cheese, and "big bowls," such as the Curry Masala and Red Lentil Dahl. There are also a variety of wrapps, sandwiches, salads, and soups. Try the signature Cinnamon Knot, mango cheesecake, or chocolate macadamia pecan pie.

Bread Garden Bakery & Cafe

110 - 100 Schoolhouse Street
SCHOOLHOUSE
604-515-0295

Map: 8
Reference: 44
Hours: M-Th 6am - 11pm,
F & Sat 6am - 12am,
Sun 6am - 11pm
Coffee: JJ Bean
Clientele: students, locals
Ambience: casual

Coquitlam

Death By Chocolate

1039 - 1163 Pinetree Way
PINETREE
604-468-0246

Map: 8
Reference: 45
Hours: M-F 8am - 12am
Sat 9am - 12am,
Sun 11am - 12am
Coffee: Seattle's Best Coffee
Clientele: chocolate and ice cream lovers and coffee connoisseurs
Ambience: art deco

At Coquitlam's Death By Chocolate, the presentation is part of the experience. Watch expert pastry chefs create one of the thirty unique 'custom-designed' dessert creations. A few of the most popular include "Between The Sheets," "Latin Lover," "Ebony & Ivory," "Multitude Of Sins" and "Crumble In My Arms." There is a long list of sandwiches and baked goods, such as muffins, cookies, and dessert bars, and many espresso drinks from which to choose.

Gallagher's Espresso Bar

102 - 1032 Austin Avenue
AUSTIN HEIGHTS
604-931-2326

Map: 8
Reference: 46
Hours: M-Sat 6am - 11pm,
Sun 7am - 10pm
Coffee: Seattle's Best Coffee
Clientele: families, students, and businesspeople
Ambience: feels just like home

Located in Coquitlam's Austin Heights neighborhood, Gallagher's Espresso Bar is filled with antique tables, leather chairs, live music and candles to create the feeling of being at home. Food selections feature a wide variety of paninis, wrapps, burritos, pizza, cold salads, sandwiches, soups, quiche, and lasagna. There are lots of desserts, including cakes and pies, from chocolate pecan to mixed fruit.

Coquitlam

Starbucks

2991 Lougheed Highway
PINETREE
604-944-8032

Map: 8
Reference: 47
Hours: 5:30am - 11pm, Sun 6am - 11pm
Coffee: Starbucks
Clientele: locals
Ambience: busy

Located in Pine Tree Shopping Center, this cafe offers all of Starbucks' coffee and tea blends. Among the most popular are the "Frappuccino," a creamy, low-fat blend of coffee, milk, and other flavours customized with your choice of mocha, espresso, caramel or syrups. The "Latte Macchiato" has steamed milk topped with foam and marked with a ristretto shot ("short pull") poured through the centre of the drink. Food selection includes sandwiches, baked goods and desserts.

Child-Friendly Cafes

Feel the need to indulge yourself in a gourmet coffee but don't want to leave your kids at home? Why not visit a "child-friendly" cafe that offers menus and a wide variety of activities to entertain children while parents can enjoy a hot beverage. The following places have many features of interest to kids and adults alike. Check the index in the back for locations and neighborhood maps.

Grab-a-Java
Unit 2 - 33093 7th Avenue, Mission, Phone: 604-826-5282
Features: children love the ice cream, shakes, and hot chocolate

La Solace Café
4883 Mackenzie Street, Vancouver, Phone: 604-266-4029
Features: toys, books

Solly's Bagelry
189 East 28th Avenue, Vancouver, Phone: 604-872-1821
Features: kid's art exhibition every month

Sweet Tooth Cafe
2404 East Hastings Street, Vancouver, Phone: 604-255-6997
Features: children's menu

Turk's Coffee House
1276 Commercial Drive, Vancouver, Phone: 604-255-5805
Features: toys, books

Map 9
Surrey, Langley
& White Rock

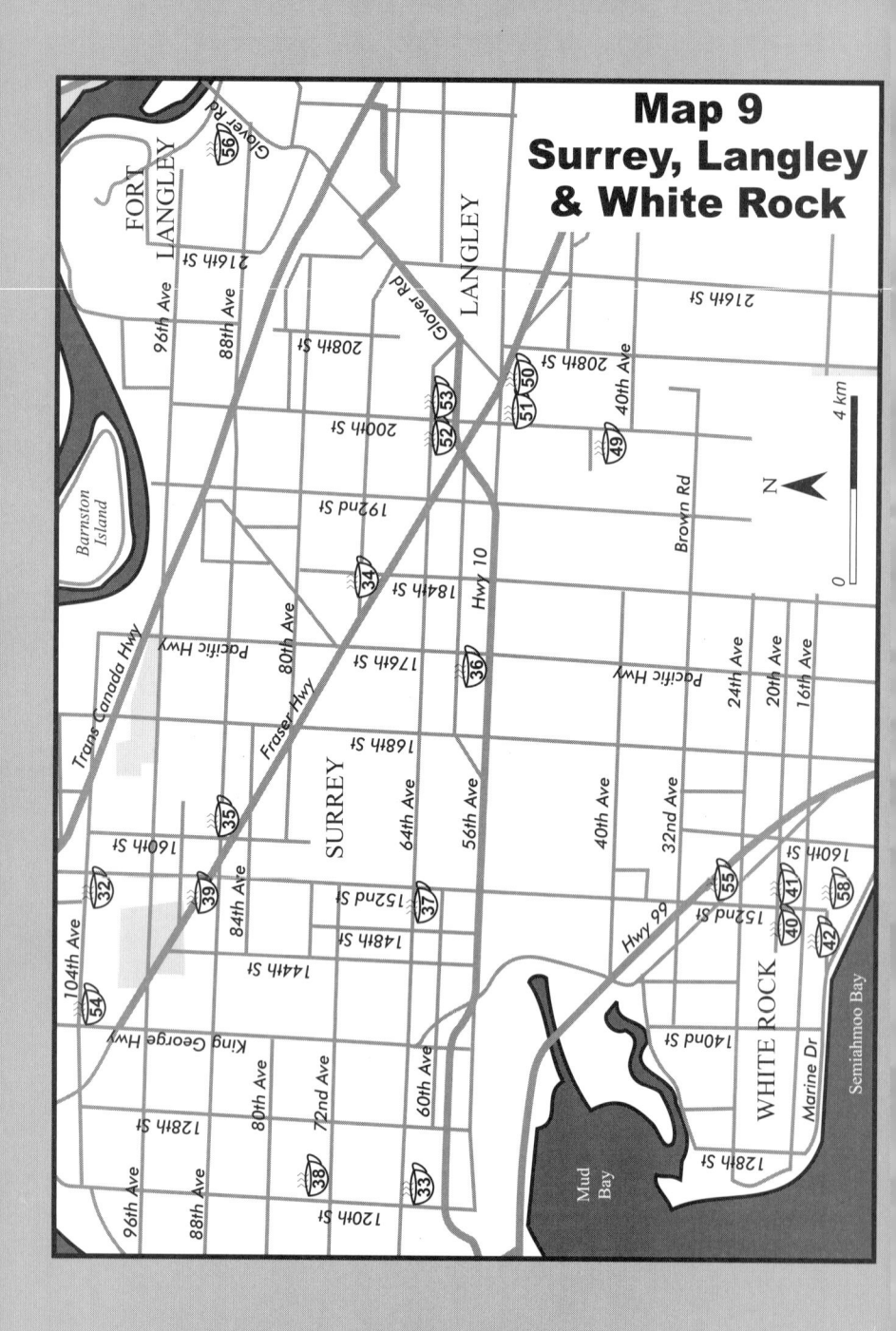

Surrey

Extending all the way from the Fraser River to Boundary Bay and the U.S. border, Surrey is situated southeast of Vancouver and between Delta to the west and Langley to the east. A rapidly growing residential and business region, Surrey is comprised of many diverse communities from Whalley and Guildford in the northwest parts, the main business and shopping districts of Surrey, down through Fleetwood, Newton, Cloverdale and South Surrey. Each has its own character, so tour around and enjoy the cafes.

Surrey

Bread Garden Bakery & Cafe

Guilford Town Centre
GUILDFORD
604-589-8859

Map: 9
Reference: 32
Hours: M-Sun 7am - 12am
Coffee: JJ Bean
Clientele: shoppers, and locals
Ambience: cozy and comfortable

Bread Garden at Guildford Town Centre offers a large selection of high quality fresh foods and beverages. The menu includes roasted vegetable lasagna, smoked salmon quiche, noodles & cheese, and "big bowls," such as the Curry Masala and Red Lentil Dahl. There are also a variety of wrapps, sandwiches, salads, and soups. Try the chocolate cake, or chocolate macadamia pecan pie.

Cravings Coffee & Bakery

147 - 6350 120th Street
NEWTON
604-502-9544

Map: 9
Reference: 33
Hours: M-F 6am - 7pm, Sat & Sun 8am - 6pm
Coffee: Crown
Clientele: everyone
Ambience: casual, warm, inviting

At 54th and Scott Road in Surrey's Newton area, Cravings Coffee & Bakery is a place to relax and enjoy a fine beverage. Each item on the menu is freshly made. There are soups, sandwiches, salads and desserts. Sandwiches include roast beef, turkey and Tuna. For dessert, try the house favourite pecan pie or one of the nearly two dozen varieties of homemade muffins.

Surrey

Esquires Coffee House

16011 Fraser Highway
FLEETWOOD
604-599-8987

Map: 9
Reference: 35
Hours: M-F 5:45am - 10pm
Coffee: Canterbury
Clientele: commuters, office workers
Ambience: relaxing

In Fleetwood, Esquires Coffee House was recently renovated and continues to serve piping hot coffee, as well as teas and other beverages to morning commuters on route to work, afternoon customers who drop by to meet their friends, and evening strollers who come by for a snack. The menu includes an assortment of tempting dishes, from fresh calzones, quiche, wrapps, and sausage rolls, to pastries and pies.

The Junction Magazine & Coffee House

5667 176th Street
CLOVERDALE
604-576-9476

Map: 9
Reference: 36
Hours: M-F 8:30am - 6pm.
Sat 9am - 5pm,
Sun 11am - 4pm
Coffee: Boyd's
Clientele: huge range
Ambience: comfortable

The Junction serves fresh coffee drinks and snacks while offering a huge selection of magazines at its location on "Antique Row" in Cloverdale. Here you can also play a game of Keno. Muffins and sweets complement the beverages and magazines.

Surrey

Java Hut Espresso Co.

301 - 6361 152nd Street
CLOVERDALE
604-572-3326

Map: 9
Reference: 37
Hours: M-F 5:30am - 11pm, Sat 6:30am - 11pm, Sun 7am - 11pm
Coffee: JJ Bean
Clientele: office commuters, locals
Ambience: Caribbean decor and cozy

This bustling neighborhood cafe is popular among Cloverdale residents and office commuters. A variety of hot and cold lunch and dessert items, including cheesecake, fruit pies, and muffins are on the menu at this upbeat and friendly place known for its Caribbean atmosphere.

Starbucks @ Chapters

100 - 12101 72nd Avenue
NEWTON
604-502-7188

Map: 9
Reference: 38
Hours: M-Sun 9am -11pm
Coffee: Starbucks
Clientele: businesspeople
Ambience: upbeat

You'll find Starbucks' coffee and tea blends all over Surrey. Try the "Caffe Latte," steamed milk with a rich shot of espresso, topped with foamed milk, or the "Frappuccino," a creamy, low-fat blend of coffee and milk, custom-made with your choice of mocha, espresso, caramel or syrups. The "Latte Macchiato" contains steamed milk topped with foam and marked with a ristretto shot ("short pull") poured through the centre of the drink. Food selections include sandwiches, baked goods and desserts.

Surrey

Starbucks

8898 152nd Street
FLEETWOOD
604-951-9373

Map: 9
Reference: 39
Hours: M-F 6am - 10pm,
Sat 10:30am - 6pm,
Sun 7am - 10pm
Coffee: Starbucks
Clientele: businesspeople and locals
Ambience: comfortable

Starbucks

10362 King George Highway
WHALLEY
604-581-2632

Map: 9
Reference: 54
Hours: M-Th 5:30am - 10:30pm, F 5:30am - 11pm, Sat 6:30am - 11pm, Sun 6:30am - 10:30pm
Coffee: Starbucks
Clientele: businesspeople and locals
Ambience: busy

120

White Rock

White Rock is situated in the southwest corner of the Lower Mainland, near the Canada/US border. A commercial and residential seaside community known for its long sandy beach, heritage pier, train station, and extended red brick waterfront promenade, White Rock is lined with galleries, boutiques, and sidewalk cafes. Marine Drive is the main access road through the city, which overlooks Boundary Bay. In the eastern part of White Rock, next to the southern points of Surrey, is the Semiahmoo Shopping Centre. It attracts many locals and American tourists. Visit a cafe and enjoy White Rock's beautiful scenery.

White Rock

Bread Garden Bakery & Cafe

1601-152nd Street
SEMIAHMOO
604-531-8324

Map: 9
Reference: 40
Hours: M-Sun 6am - 10pm
Coffee: JJ Bean
Clientele: locals, shoppers, and tourists
Ambience: cozy and comfortable

White Rock's Bread Garden, located in Semiahmoo Shopping Centre, offers a large selection of high quality fresh foods and beverages. The menu features roasted vegetable lasagna, smoked salmon quiche, noodles & cheese, and "big bowls," such as the Curry Masala and Red Lentil Dahl. There are also a variety of wrapps, sandwiches, salads, and soups. Try the mango cheesecake, or chocolate macadamia pecan pie.

Starbucks

15355 24th Avenue
WHITE ROCK
604-531-0774

Map: 9
Reference: 55
Hours: M-F 5:30am - 10pm, Sat & Sun 6am - 10pm
Coffee: Starbucks
Clientele: locals and shoppers
Ambience: relaxing

You'll find all of Starbucks' coffee and tea blends in White Rock. Try the "Caffe Latte," steamed milk with a rich shot of espresso, topped with foamed milk, or the "Frappuccino," a creamy, low-fat blend of coffee and milk, customized with mocha, espresso, caramel or syrups. The "Latte Macchiato" contains steamed milk topped with foam and marked with a ristretto shot ("short pull") poured through the centre of the drink. Food selections include sandwiches, baked goods and desserts.

White Rock

Starbucks

1730 - 152nd Street
SEMIAHMOO
604-541-1170

Map: 9
Reference: 41
Hours: M-F 5:30am - 10pm,
Sat & Sun 6am - 10pm
Coffee: Starbucks
Clientele: locals and shoppers
Ambience: upbeat

Whitby's Bookstore & Coffee House

14837 Marine Drive
MARINE
604-536-3711

Map: 9
Reference: 42
Hours: M-Sun 7am - 10pm
Coffee: Canterbury & Coloiera
Clientele: professionals, book enthusiasts
Ambience: bright, friendly, and relaxed

Whitby's Bookstore & Coffee House was inspired by Whitby, England, an attractive tourist destination off the North Sea, full of fish and chips, ice cream shops, and a scenic pier just like White Rock. At Whitby's browse the book stacks, enjoy a specialty coffee or tea, and sample a snack. There's a full espresso and juice bar complemented by freshly baked muffins, scones, bagels, homemade soups, fresh salads, wrapps, and sandwiches on focaccia or multi-grain bread. For rich desserts, try some pie. Lemon meringue and the bumbleberry are among the most tempting.

Teahouses

If you're not much of a coffee drinker or want a non-coffee-based beverage for a change of pace, try a teahouse and broaden your horizons while experiencing some unique flavours! Though almost every cafe sells tea, the following establishments specialize in a wide range of common and exotic tea blends along with light meals.

Clancy's Tea Cosy

15223 Pacific Avenue
WHITE ROCK
604-541-9010

Map: 9
Reference: 58
Hours: M-Sun 11am - 4:30pm
Tea Varieties: 35 - 40
Clientele: locals and tourists
Ambience: soothing

At Johnson & Pacific in White Rock, Clancy's Tea Cosy provides casual elegance for an enjoyable afternoon. Drop by for traditional "Afternoon Tea," accompanied by a variety of homemade soups, light lunches and freshly baked scones and desserts. Also available for sale are packaged teas, teapots and tea accessories.

Secret Garden Tea Company

5559 West Boulevard
KERRISDALE
604-261-3070

Map: 3
Reference: 50
Hours: M-Sat 8am - 7pm, Sun 9am - 6pm
Tea Varieties: 45
Clientele: locals, all ages
Ambience: elegant and serene

In a peaceful environment enhanced by live harp music in the heart of Vancouver's West Side, Secret Garden Tea Company serves traditional "High Tea," where a variety of homemade foods, from pastries and assorted finger sandwiches to scones with Devon cream and jam, are served.

Teahouses

T

1568 West Broadway
SOUTH GRANVILLE
604-878-3000

Map: 3
Reference: 51
Hours: M-Th 9:30am - 7pm, F 9:30am - 11pm, Sat 11am - 11pm, Sun 11am - 6pm
Tea Varieties: 150
Clientele: tea connoisseurs
Ambience: "architectural minimalism meets Japanese tearoom culture"

At Granville and Broadway tea experts and novices feel at home at T. An upscale oasis, T is stacked from floor to ceiling with over 150 varieties of tea from which to choose. Enjoy some scones, cookies, and tea treats. T blends its own tea and sells wholesale tea to restaurants and hotels across North America.

Langley

Langley is located east of Surrey, west of Aldergrove, south of the Fraser River, and north of the US border. A vast area, "Langley" is actually comprised of a city, township, and an old fort. While Langley City is a distinct district of its own, the Township of Langley is a large municipality that governs many communities, including Fort Langley, Brookswood, and Willowbrook. Fort Langley, the historic capital of the province, is a unique place with many heritage buildings, antique dealers, and restaurants. Popular among tourists and locals, there is a lot to see and do in this historic region of Greater Vancouver. Wherever you happen to go in Langley, stop by a cafe for a thirst-quenching break.

Langley

Cravings Coffee & Bakery

4061 200th Street
LANGLEY CITY
604-533-5596

Map: 9
Reference: 49
Hours: M-F 6am - 9pm, Sat & Sun 7:30am - 7pm
Coffee: Crown
Clientele: everyone
Ambience: warm, cozy and inviting

Throughout Langley, Cravings Coffee & Bakery provides a place to relax and enjoy a fine beverage. Each item on the menu is freshly made. There are soups, sandwiches, salads and desserts. Sandwiches include roast beef, turkey and Tuna. For dessert, try the house favourite pecan pie or one of the nearly two dozen varieties of homemade muffins.

Cravings Coffee & Bakery

104 - 20436 Fraser Highway
LANGLEY CITY
604-530-5547

Map: 9
Reference: 50
Hours: M-F 6am - 9pm, Sat & Sun 7:30am - 7pm
Coffee: Crown
Clientele: everyone
Ambience: casual, warm, inviting

Langley

Cravings Coffee & Bakery

102 - 5499 203rd Street
BROOKSWOOD
604-533-5309

Map: 9
Reference: 51
Hours: M-F 6am - 9pm,
Sat & Sun 7:30am - 7pm
Coffee: Crown
Clientele: everyone
Ambience: busy

Langley

Starbucks

107 - 6153 200th Street
WILLOWBROOK
604-530-1340

Map: 9
Reference: 52
Hours: M-F 6am - 10:30pm, Sat & Sun 8am -10:30pm
Coffee: Starbucks
Clientele: shoppers and locals
Ambience: comfortable and upbeat

Langley's Starbucks' locations offer all of Starbucks' coffee and tea blends. Try the "Caffe Latte," steamed milk with a rich shot of espresso, topped with foamed milk, or the "Frappuccino," a creamy, low-fat blend of coffee and milk, customized with mocha, espresso, caramel or syrups. The "Latte Macchiato" contains steamed milk topped with foam and marked with a ristretto shot ("short pull") poured through the centre of the drink. Enjoy some baked goods and desserts.

Starbucks @ Chapters

105 - 20015 Langley By-Pass
LANGLEY CITY
604-514-2315

Map: 9
Reference: 53
Hours: M-Sun 9am - 11pm
Coffee: Starbucks
Clientele: shoppers, locals, and book enthusiasts
Ambience: comfortable

Langley

Wendel's Books & Café

103 - 9233 Glover Road
FORT LANGLEY
604-513-2238

Map: 9
Reference: 56
Hours: M-Sun 7:30am - 10pm
Coffee: Torrefazione Italia
Clientele: people who appreciate high quality and fresh products
Ambience: Refined, earthy, inviting and relaxed

In the village of Fort Langley, Wendel's Books & Café is a gathering place for locals and tourists alike. Named after the owner's grandfather, Wendel's offers an espresso bar, fresh baking, and a full breakfast and lunch menu with different daily specials for dinner all within a full-service bookstore. There is a heated patio that overlooks the gardens of the historic site of a train station. The cafe offers foods with ethnic influences like Asian, Mediterranean, German, and Mexican. For breakfast try the Belgian Waffle, Samosa Pie, Black Bean Quesadilla, or Falafel Wrapp. For lunch there is an assortment of sandwiches, wrapps, salads, burgers, and tapas. Dinners feature grilled fish, chicken, pastas and vegetarian dishes. Desserts vary from day to day, but are all freshly made on the premises. Some of the standards include chocolate cake, bread pudding, peanut butter pie, apple pie, and coffee-iced cinnamon buns. Beverages include chai tea and coffees, all available with regular milk or soymilk, fresh juice bar, yogurt smoothies, frappes and bottled drinks. Catering is also available. Buy some coffee beans to take home. Wendel's will grind them to suit whatever type of brewing equipment you have in your kitchen or office.

Map 10
Whistler

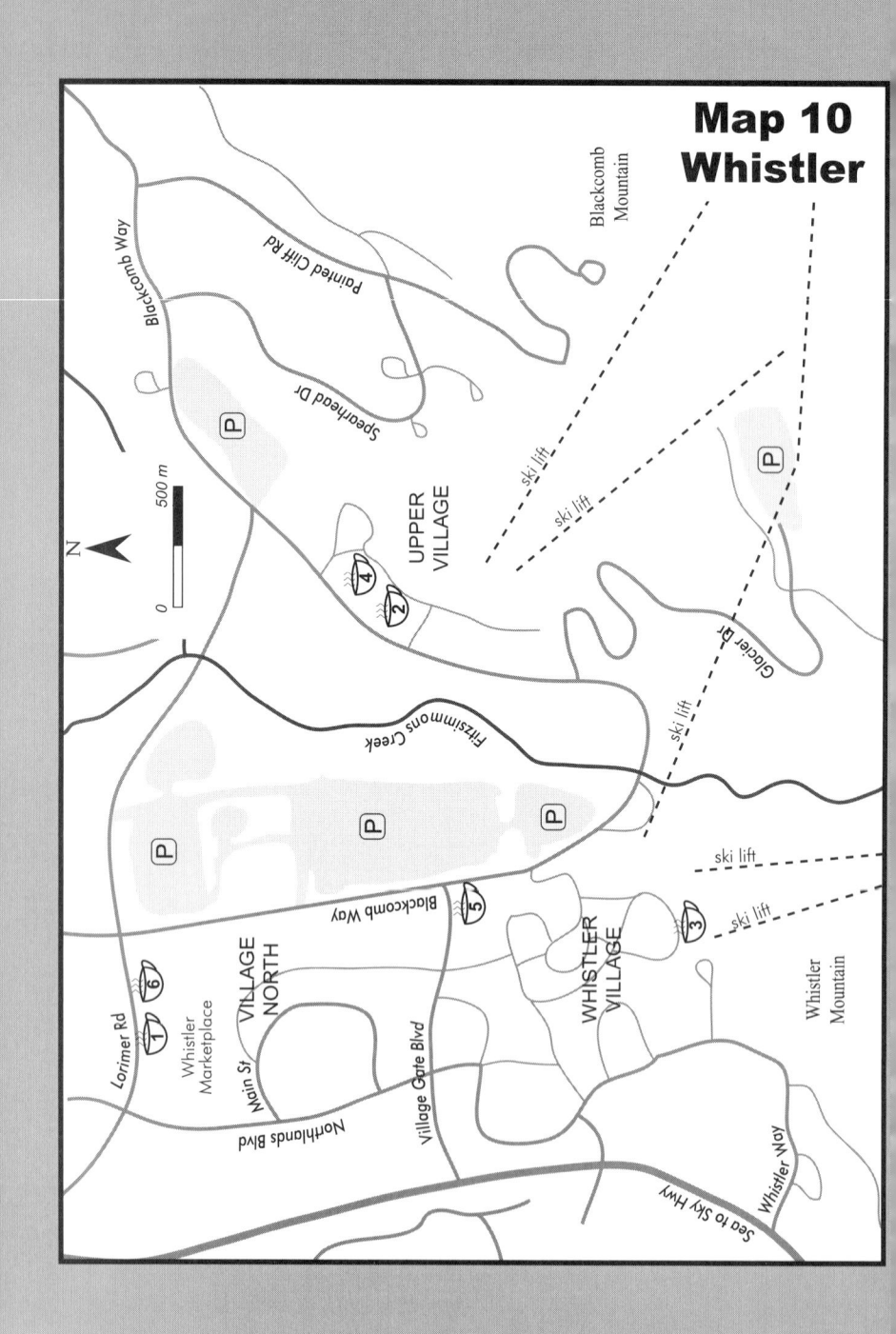

Whistler

In winter, Whistler and Blackcomb Mountains offer among the best skiing and snowboarding anywhere. In summer, this region is still a great place to be, whether for a weekend getaway or an extended stay. Regardless of the time of year, don't forget to visit Whistler-area cafes! You'll find them in Whistler's Marketplace, Whistler Village and Blackcomb's Upper Village. So, whether you prefer skiing, boarding, hiking, biking or just plain lounging, enjoy a cup of hot chocolate, cafe mocha, or some hot or iced tea.

Whistler

Auntie Em's Kitchen

129 - 4340 Lorimer Road
MARKETPLACE
604-932-1163

Map: 10
Reference: 1
Hours: M-Sun 6:30am - 6pm
Coffee: Coloiera
Clientele: tourists and locals
Ambience: cozy and bright

In the Marketplace at Main Street and Northlands Boulevard, Auntie Em's Kitchen makes breakfasts all day long. Healthy food is the goal with vegetarian soups, homemade bread, sandwiches, and baked goods on the menu. Stop by on your way to or from your Whistler activities and have a beverage along with one of the daily specials.

Chef Bernard's Cafe

1 - 4573 Chateau Boulevard
UPPER VILLAGE
604-932-7051

Map: 10
Reference: 2
Hours: M-Th 7am - 7pm, F - Sun 7am - 10pm
Coffee: JJ Bean
Clientele: Whistler residents, tourists, and resort staff
Ambience: casual

Located across from Blackomb's Chateau Whistler Resort in the Upper Village, this casual cafe features local organic ingredients in all of Chef Bernard's cooking. Complete breakfasts, lunches and dinners are served. Try one of the cinnamon buns with a coffee.

Whistler

Death By Chocolate

4174 Springs Lane
WHISTLER VILLAGE
604-938-1323

Map: 10
Reference: 3
Hours: M-Sun 7am - 12am
Coffee: Seattle's Best Coffee
Clientele: chocolate and ice cream lovers and coffee connoisseurs
Ambience: art deco

Experience the presentation at Death By Chocolate, just around the corner from Whistler's gondola. Watch expert pastry chefs create one of the thirty unique 'custom-designed' dessert creations. A few of the most popular include "Between The Sheets," "Latin Lover," "Ebony & Ivory," "Multitude Of Sins" and "Crumble In My Arms." There is a long list of sandwiches and baked goods, such as muffins, cookies, and dessert bars, and many espresso drinks

Portobello

4599 Chateau Boulevard
UPPER VILLAGE
604-938-2040

Map: 10
Reference: 4
Hours: M-Sun 7am - 10pm
Coffee: Torrefazione Italia
Clientele: hotel guests, locals and visitors
Ambience: country atmosphere

A market-style restaurant with an "open kitchen concept," Portobello offers soups, sandwiches, salads, pastas, pizza, seafood, Chef's daily specials, and vegetarian selections either inside or at the outdoor take-out window. Whether you are in search of a quick breakfast, specialty coffee, or a snack to go, come inside and order something at the Portobello Deli counter to satisfy your mountain appetite. The gift section has traditional Italian pastas, salads, olive oils, vinaigrettes, authentic Canadian maple syrups, Torrefazione coffee, and "T Room" Tea.

Whistler

Starbucks

123 - 4295 Blackcomb Way
WHISTLER VILLAGE
604-938-0611

Map: 10
Reference: 5
Hours: M-Sun 6:30am - 10pm
Coffee: Starbucks
Clientele: locals and tourists
Ambience: comfortable and upbeat

In Whistler, you'll find Starbucks' coffee and tea blends at two locations. Try some hot chocolate or the "Caffe Latte," steamed milk with a rich shot of espresso, topped with foamed milk, or the "Latte Macchiato," steamed milk topped with foam and marked with a ristretto shot ("short pull") poured through the centre of the drink. Sandwiches and muffins are always popular choices.

Starbucks

120 - 4340 Lorimer Road
VILLAGE NORTH
604-905-0833

Map: 10
Reference: 6
Hours: M-Sun 6:30am - 10pm
Coffee: Starbucks
Clientele: locals and tourists
Ambience: comfortable and upbeat

Cafes on the Internet

Blinding Light Café	www.blindinglight.com
Blenz Coffee	www.blenz.com
Bojangles Café	www.bojanglescafe.com
Boleto	www.boleto.ca
Butler Did It	www.butlerdiditcatering.com
Caffé Artigiano	www.caffeartigiano.com
Canadian Maple Delights	www.mapledelights.com
Cuppa Joe Coffee	www.cuppajoecoffee.com
Death By Chocolate	www.deathbychocolate.ca
Elysian Room	www.elysianroom.com
Esquires Coffee	www.esquirescoffee.com
Fish Café	www.fish-cafe.com
Ghiradelli	www.ghirardelli.com
Havana	www.havana-art.com
Indigo Books Café	www.chapters.indigo.ca
Java Hut Espresso	www.thejavahut.com
JJ Bean	www.jjbeancoffee.com
Junction Magazine	www.junctionmagazine.com
Meinhardt Fine Foods	www.meinhardt.com
Mondo Gelato	www.mondogelato.com
The Naam	www.thenaam.com
Panne Rizo	www.pannerizo.com
Portfolio	www.portfolioartgallery.com
Salt Spring Roasting Co.	www.saltspringroasting.com
Seattles Best Coffee	www.sbc.ca
Starbucks	www.starbucks.com
T	www.tealeaves.com
Tonys Deli	www.tonysdeli.com
Torrefazione Italia	www.titalia.com
Urban Fare	www.urbanfare.com
Virgin Megastore Café	www.virginmega.com
Whitby's Bookstore	www.whitbys.bc.ca

Map 11 Downtown Victoria

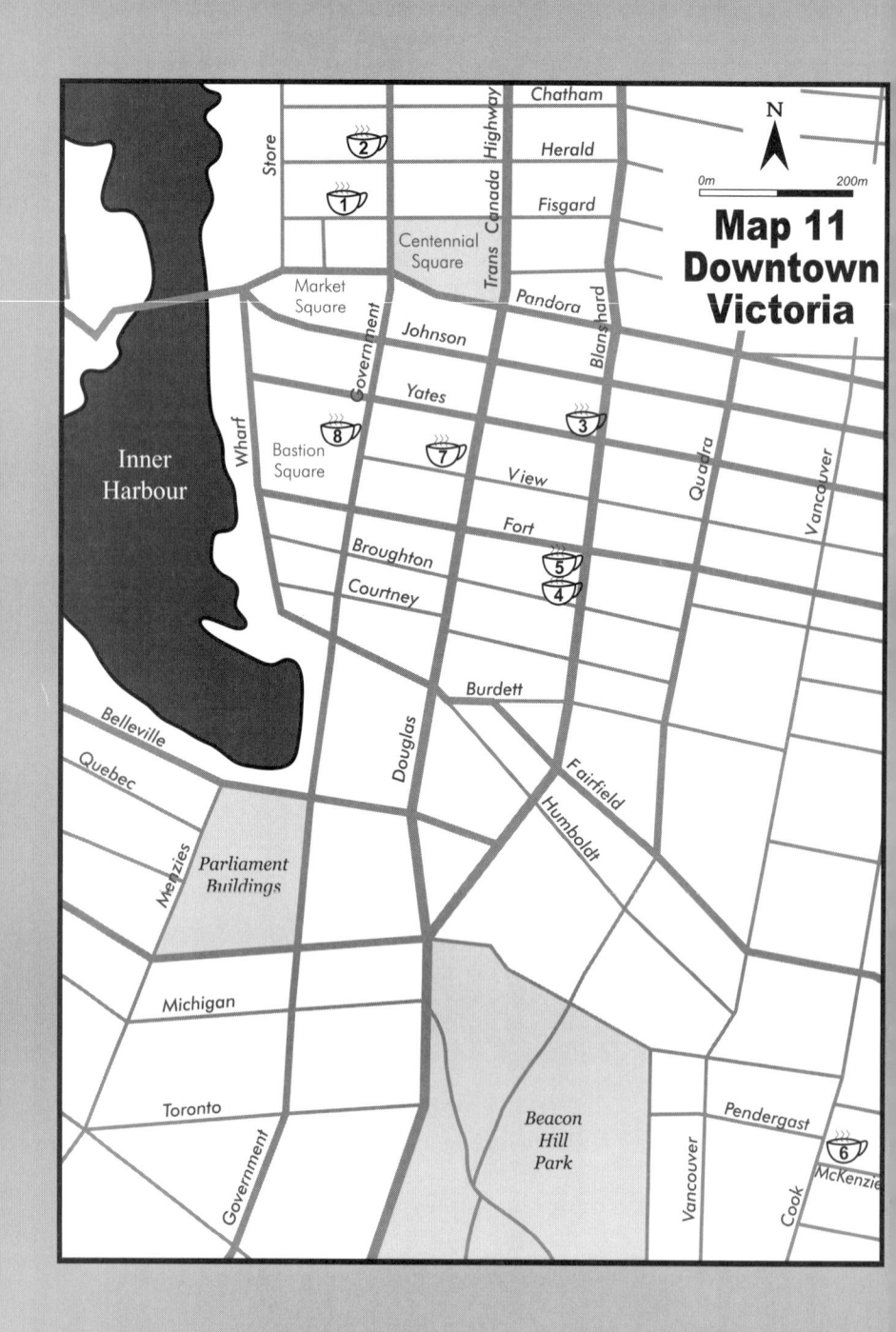

Victoria

Taking a scenic ferryboat ride through the waters of the Strait of Georgia from Tsawwassen to Swartz Bay will lead you to Victoria, the capital of British Columbia, which sits on the southern tip of Vancouver Island. A city rich in history, tourist sites, and residential neighborhoods, many cafes are centered in Victoria's downtown within walking distance of BC's impressive Parliament Buildings, the famous Empress Hotel, Beacon Hill Park, and the shoppers paradise of Eaton Centre on Government Street.

Victoria

Bean Around the World Coffees

533 Fisgard Street
DOWNTOWN
250-386-7115

Map: 11
Reference: 1
Hours: M-Sat 7am - 6pm, Sun 9am - 6pm
Coffee: Bean Around the World
Clientele: eclectic mix
Ambience: Bohemian, comfortable

Upon entering Bean Around the World, visitors are greeted by the aroma of freshly ground coffee inside a brick heritage building with tall ceilings and a mezzanine near Victoria's Chinatown. The menu features grilled sandwiches, soups and bakery items.

Cascadia Wholefoods Bakery

1812 Government Street
DOWNTOWN
250-380-6606

Map: 11
Reference: 2
Hours: M 8:30am - 3:30pm, T & W 8:30am - 8pm, Th - Sat 8:30am - 9pm, Sun 8:30am - 3:30pm
Coffee: Torrefazione Italia
Clientele: cross section
Ambience: casual and warm

Situated in 'Olde Town' on Government Street, once Victoria's shipping and commercial centre and now a tourist area with British pubs, craft and antique stores, Cascadia Wholefoods Bakery makes baked goods from scratch for its restaurant Re-Bar as well as for various Victoria landmarks. Inside the bakery, try the savory lunch items, soups, panini and Artisan hand-shaped breads.

Victoria

Demitasse Coffeebar

320 Blanshard Street
DOWNTOWN
250-386-4442

Map: 11
Reference: 3
Hours: M-F 7am - 7pm, Sat & Sun 9am - 5pm
Coffee: JJ Bean
Clientele: businesspeople and locals
Ambience: European atmosphere

At Blanshard and Johnson Streets, Demitasse Coffeebar has been serving muffins, scones, croissants, sandwiches and soups for twenty years. The "Hot Filled Croissants" are local favourites and are prepared with a choice of tomatoes, mushrooms, smoked salmon, and avocado. Try the "Bagel Melt," Edam cheese melted over tomatoes and onions on a toasted bagel. There are many salads from which to choose including Greek, Caesar, artichoke & capers, and a cold noodle salad with marinated tofu, peppers and cilantro.

Mocambo Coffee

1028 Blanshard Street
DOWNTOWN
250-384-4468

Map: 11
Reference: 4
Hours: M-Th 7am - 6pm, F 7am - 11pm, Sat 7am - 10pm
Coffee: Torrefazione Italia
Clientele: civil servants, tourists
Ambience: nice and cozy

At Mocambo local artists' works are showcased on the walls and poetry and comedy nights happen all the time to entertain Mocambo's loyal clientele and tourists. Besides the coffee, there are a wide variety of sandwiches, soups and pastries.

Victoria

Starbucks

801 Fort Street
DOWNTOWN
250-383-6208

Map: 11
Reference: 5
Hours: M-Sat 6am - 11pm, Sun 6am - 10pm
Coffee: Starbucks
Clientele: locals and tourists
Ambience: busy

In Victoria there are several Starbucks locations, including one on Fort Street, one in Chapters Bookstore on Douglas Street and one in Cook Street Village east of Beacon Hill Park. Try the "Caffe Latte," steamed milk with a rich shot of espresso, topped with foamed milk, or the "Frappuccino," a creamy, low-fat blend of coffee and milk, customized with mocha, espresso, caramel or syrups. The "Latte Macchiato" contains steamed milk topped with foam and marked with a ristretto shot ("short pull") poured through the centre of the drink. Food choices include baked goods and desserts.

Starbucks

320 Cook Street
COOK STREET VILLAGE
250-380-7606

Map: 11
Reference: 6
Hours: M-Sun 6am - 12am
Coffee: Starbucks
Clientele: locals
Ambience: relaxed

Victoria

Starbucks @ Chapters

1212 Douglas Street
DOWNTOWN
250-380-9009

Map: 11
Reference: 7
Hours: M-Sat 9am - 9pm, Sun 10am - 8pm
Coffee: Starbucks
Clientele: locals and tourists
Ambience: literate and inspiring

Torrefazione Italia

1234 Government Street
DOWNTOWN
250-920-7203

Map: 11
Reference: 8
Hours: M-Th 6:30am - 9pm, F 6:30am - 10pm, Sat 7:30am - 10pm, Sun 8:30am - 7pm
Coffee: Torrefazione Italia
Clientele: businesspeople and younger crowd
Ambience: "Warmth of Italy"

Seattle-based Torrefazione Italia provides Victoria with an elegant Italian atmosphere, complete with high ceilings, in which to enjoy a latte or cappuccino. Each month a different artist's paintings are showcased. There is a great selection of Italian sandwiches, pastries, cookies and gelati. The coffee beans come from Torrefazione's own roasting plant in Seattle.

Day Trips

It's no secret that Greater Vancouver, Victoria and Whistler are wonderful places. But they are also terrific starting points from which to travel to other great places! Each of the following cafes make for ideal resting points during an enjoyable day's excursion away from Vancouver, Victoria or Whistler.

Map 12
Mission & Abbotsford

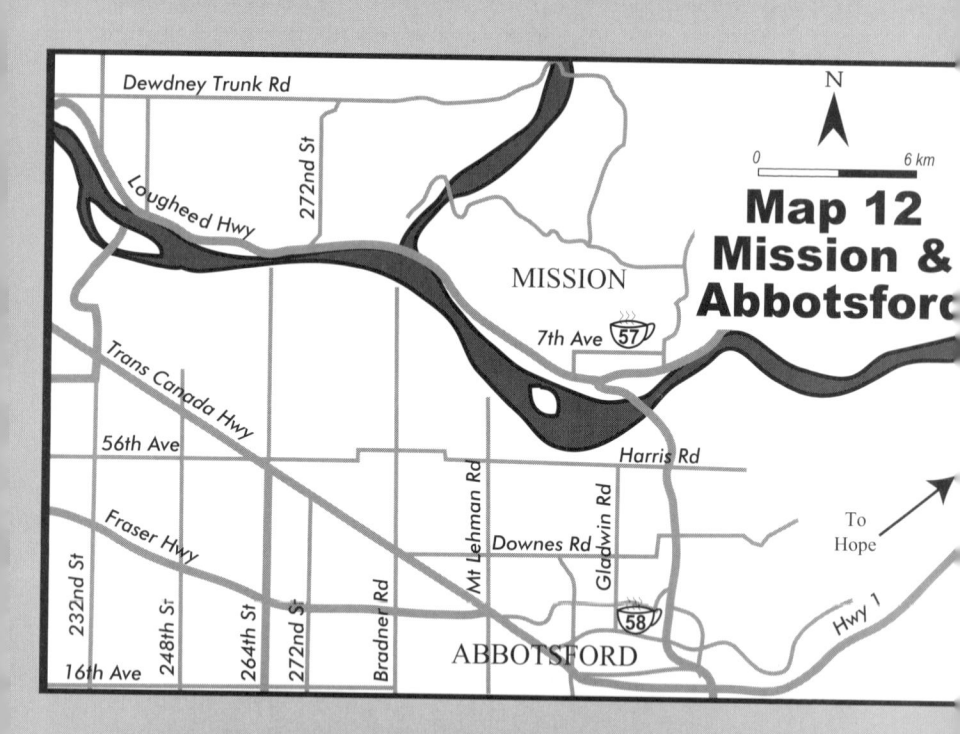

146

Mission

Traveling eastward along the Trans Canada Highway will take you to the Fraser Valley, a vast region southeast of Greater Vancouver where there are at least two worthwhile "local escapes" on the south and north side of the mighty Fraser River. On the south side of the Fraser River is Abbotsford, a farming community that has blossomed into a large urban area with "rural distractions." The famous Abbotsford International Airshow is held each August featuring all types of planes for aircraft enthusiasts. On the north side of the Fraser is Mission, historically a popular resting stop for river navigators and trappers, now a great place for sightseeing and outdoor recreation in the many surrounding lakes, parks and hiking trails. You can even visit the Mission Museum and learn about BC's past, either before or after a coffee break!

Grab-a-Java

Unit 2 - 33093 7th Avenue
MISSION
604-826-5282

Map: 12
Reference: 57
Hours: M-F 6:30am - 10pm,
Sat 7am -10pm,
Sun 8am - 10pm
Coffee: Torrefazione Italia
Clientele: families, business and arts crowds
Ambience: A warm "in your living room" feeling

This self-described "funky cafe" offers a variety of freshly baked items, such as scones, muffins, and cinnamon buns as well as wrapps and custom sandwiches. Children love the ice cream, shakes, and hot chocolate. Parents love the coffee. The heated and covered outdoor patio has plenty of seating.

Grab-a-Java

101 - 2760 Gladwin Road
ABBOTSFORD
604-870-8610

Map: 12
Reference: 58
Hours: M-F 7am - 11:30pm,
Sat & Sun 8am - 11:30pm
Coffee: Torrefazione Italia

Map 13
Sidney &
Salt Spring Island

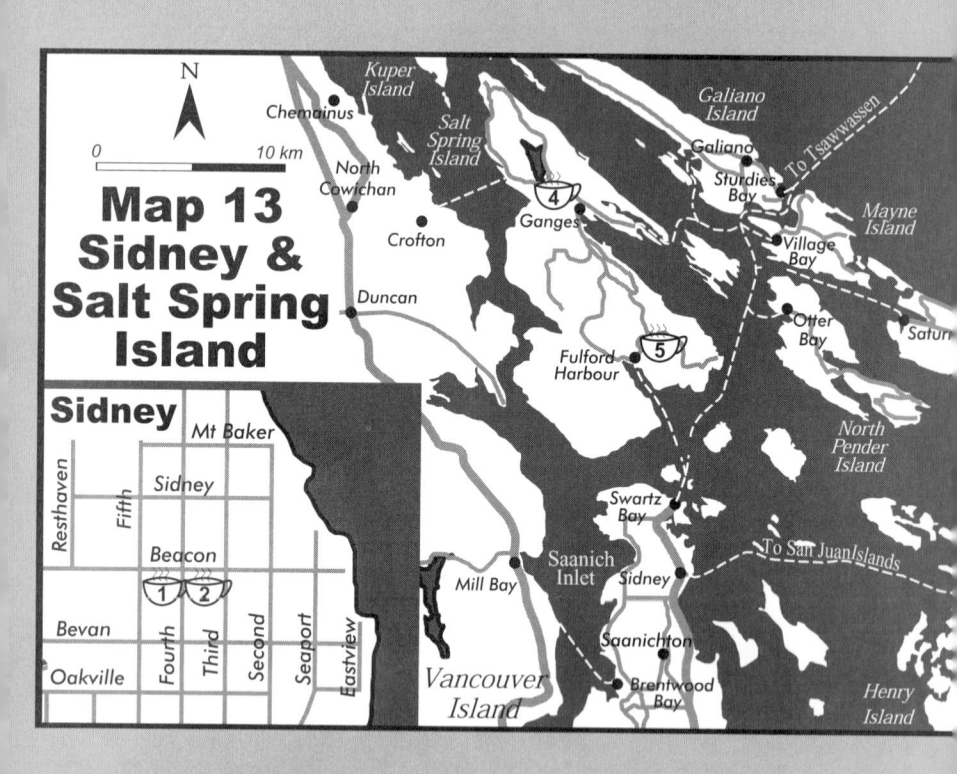

Sidney

On Vancouver Island 2 km south of Swartz Bay, this charming seaside town is a large scenic community on the eastern shore of the Saanich Peninsula. Downtown Sidney has marinas, shops, and cafes to keep you entertained.

Java Jasmine Coffeehouse

106 - 2423 Beacon Avenue
250-655-1111
SIDNEY

Map: 13
Reference: 1
Hours: M-Fri 7am - 9pm, Sat & Sun 8am - 10pm
Coffee: Torrefazione Italia
Clientele: tourists and locals
Ambience: relaxed, warm and European

Freshly baked muffins, cookies, scones, and pies are available everyday at Java Jasmine. European treats include Florentines and biscotti. Lunch fare features soup, hot panini sandwiches, frozen yogurt and fresh fruit smoothies. Granita cold drinks and selection of cold beverages, such as iced latte and iced mocha are available. The signature drink is the "Caramel Mocha Dream." Live music in summer.

Starbucks

2471 Beacon Avenue
250-655-0949
SIDNEY

Map: 13
Reference: 2
Hours: M-W 6am-10pm, Th-Sun 6am-11pm
Coffee: Starbucks
Clientele: locals and tourists
Ambience: comfortable

Located near the beach, this cafe offers all of Starbucks' coffee and tea blends. Try the ever-popular "Caffe Latte," steamed milk with a rich shot of espresso, topped with foamed milk, or the "Frappuccino," a creamy, low-fat blend of coffee and milk, customized with mocha, espresso, caramel or syrups. Baked goods and desserts are served.

Salt Spring Island

The Gulf Islands between Greater Vancouver and southern Vancouver Island are a popular diversion for tourists and locals alike. Salt Spring Island, the most visited of all the major Gulf Islands, is a tranquil and scenic place that can be reached by BC Ferries every day from either Tsawwassen or Swartz Bay. Ferries link Fulford Harbour in south Salt Spring to Swartz Bay, and Vesuvius in west Salt Spring to Crofton on Vancouver Island. Ferries from Long Harbour in east Salt Spring sail to Tsawwassen. Known for its natural beauty, art galleries, shops, restaurants, even sheep herding, Salt Spring Island is well worth a day's trip to explore. In the middle of the Island is the village of Ganges, where most shops, galleries and services can be found, including a tourist information office. Regardless of where you go on the Island don't forget to enjoy some refreshments at one of the Island's cafes.

Salt Spring Roasting Co.

109 McPhillips Avenue
GANGES
250-537-0825

Map: 13
Reference: 4
Hours: M-Sat 6am - 7pm, Sun 8am - 7pm
Coffee: Salt Spring Roasting Co.
Clientele: Island residents and tourists
Ambience: busy

In Salt Spring's Village Centre, Salt Spring Island Roasting Co. serves coffee brews made from organic, 'fair trade', coffee beans it roasts on the Island. Children love the hot cougar cocoa (complete with gummy bears on top!) while "adults" enjoy the other hot and cold beverages. Food items include cakes, pies, cookies, scones, muffins, salads, savory snacks, soups, quiche and pizza. Enjoy ongoing variety of local art on display. Bulk coffee and tea is also available for purchase.

Salt Spring Island

Salt Spring Roasting Co.

107 Morningside Road
FULFORD
250-653-2388

Map: 13
Reference: 5
Hours: M-Sat 6am - 7pm, Sun 8am - 7pm
Coffee: Salt Spring Roasting
Clientele: Island community and tourists
Ambience: comfortable

Offering the same rich menu, amenities and art exhibits as the Ganges location, enjoy a refreshing beverage and snack at Salt Spring Roasting Co.'s Fulford Harbour location.

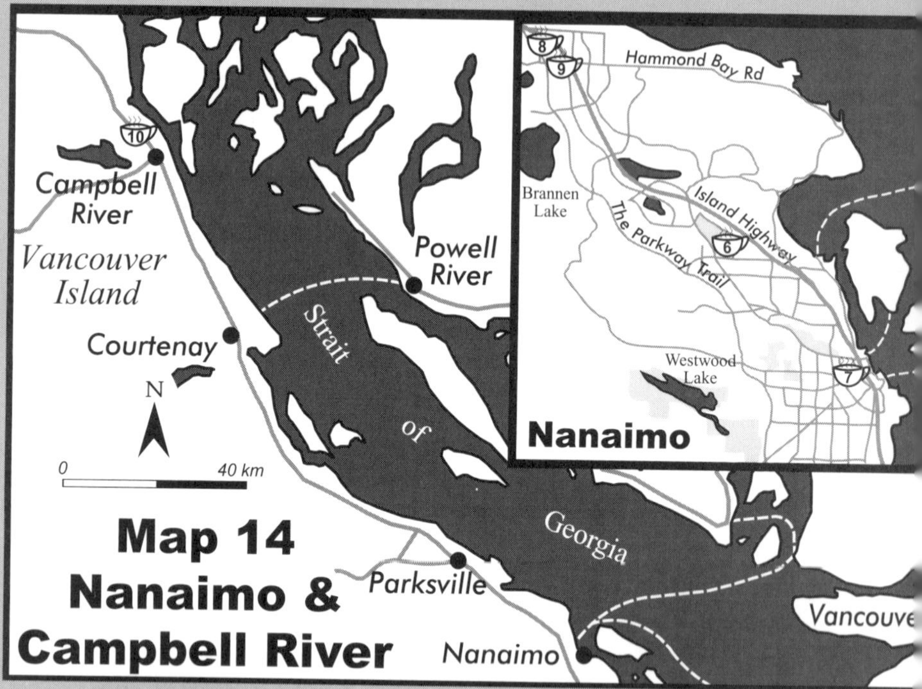
Hammond Bay Rd
Brannen Lake
Island Highway
The Parkway Trail
Westwood Lake
Nanaimo
Campbell River
Vancouver Island
Powell River
Courtenay
Strait of Georgia
N
0
40 km
Map 14
Nanaimo &
Campbell River
Parksville
Nanaimo
Vancouve

Nanaimo

A short ferryboat ride from Horseshoe Bay in West Vancouver across the Strait of Georgia takes passengers to the city of Nanaimo, a large community on the east side of central Vancouver Island, roughly 110 km north of Victoria via Highway 1. Vancouver Island's second biggest city after Victoria, Nanaimo is known for its beautiful harbour, many parks, outdoor recreation, and city shopping. A two-hour drive further north up the Inland Island Highway will bring you to picturesque Campbell River not only famous as the "Salmon Capital of the World" but also known for its many totem poles and summer whale-watching tours. A visit to Nanaimo or Campbell River is not complete without some refreshments at one of the many cafes.

Java Expressions

2A - 2220 Bowen Road
NANAIMO
250-751-0116

Map: 14
Reference: 6
Hours: M-F 6:30am - 9pm, Sat & Sun 7am - 6pm
Coffee: Organic House Blend
Clientele: families, students, tourists, and businesspeople
Ambience: relaxing

At Northfield and Bowen Road in central Nanaimo, Java Expressions serves organic coffees from beans roasted in small batches onsite and baked goods, including muffins, cinnamon buns, scones and cheesecakes, freshly made in-store daily. There are also light lunch items. Besides coffee, Java Expressions offers a large selection of herbal, green and black teas.

Nanaimo

Café Vinifera

4270 Fritzwilliam Street
NANAIMO
250-753-1797

Map: 14
Reference: 7
Hours: M-F 7am - 10pm, Sat 8am - 10pm, Sun 8am - 6pm
Coffee: Torrefazione Italia
Clientele: families
Ambience: everyone knows everyone

Café Vinifera (also known as "Bocca" by locals) is located in Nanaimo's Old City Quarter and features foods from around the world as well as "wheat-free" baking. Some menu favourites include eggplant parmigiana, blackbean enchiladas, and wheat-free Belgian chocolate brownies. Since you're in town, don't forget the Nanaimo bars! Painting and sculptures are displayed by local and international artists.

Starbucks @ Chapters

6670 Mary Ellen Drive
NANAIMO
250-390-9094

Map: 14
Reference: 8
Hours: M-Sat 6am - 9pm, Sun 7am - 9pm
Coffee: Starbucks
Clientele: locals and tourists
Ambience: comfortable and upbeat

In Nanaimo and Campbell River, you'll find all of Starbucks' coffee and tea blends. Baked goods and desserts are complemented by the many beverage choices, including "Caffe Latte," steamed milk with a rich shot of espresso, topped with foamed milk, or the "Frappuccino," a creamy, low-fat blend of coffee and milk, customized with mocha, espresso, caramel or syrups. The "Latte Macchiato" contains steamed milk topped with foam and marked with a ristretto shot ("short pull") poured through the centre of the drink.

Nanaimo

Starbucks

6631 Island Highway
NANAIMO
250-390-3835

Map: 14
Reference: 9
Hours: M-F 6am - 9pm, Sat & Sun 7am - 9pm
Coffee: Starbucks
Clientele: locals and tourists
Ambience: relaxing

Starbucks

136 - 1416 Island Highway
CAMPBELL RIVER
250-286-6335

Map: 14
Reference: 10
Hours: M-F 6am - 10pm, Sat & Sun 7am - 10pm
Coffee: Starbucks
Clientele: locals and tourists
Ambience: relaxing and quiet

Cafe Beverage Glossary

Barista - Literally, "bartender" in Italian, the term refers to a person who prepares espresso-based beverages

Breve ("Espresso Breve") - An espresso with light cream

Café au Lait - French style, an espresso beverage made with equal parts of hot coffee and steamed milk

Caffe Affogato - Literally, "drowned" in Italian, refers to hot espresso over a scoop of vanilla gelato

Caffe Americano - A shot or two of espresso poured into a glass with hot water

Caffe con Panna (or "Espresso con Panna") - Espresso topped with a spoonful of whipped cream

Caffe Freddo - Chilled espresso served in a glass, often with ice

Caffe Latte - An espresso made with steamed milk, topped with foamed milk. Contains more milk than a cappuccino

Caffe Mocha (or simply, "Mocha") - A latte with either chocolate syrup or steamed chocolate milk. May be topped with whipped cream and cocoa powder or chocolate shavings

Cappuccino - A shot of espresso topped with foamed milk with less milk than a latte

Chai - A spiced strong black tea made with milk and sugar

Doppio - A double shot of espresso

Cafe Beverage Glossary

Espresso - Literally, "quick" in Italian, a strong coffee brewed by forcing steam under pressure through darkly roasted, ground coffee beans. No milk, just coffee!

Espresso Lungo - A shot of espresso pulled long to get the most from the coffee bean, producing either a stronger espresso or a bitter cup

Espresso Macchiato - Espresso with a dollop of steamed milk on top

Espresso Ristretto - Literally, "restricted" in Italian, refers to a shot of espresso pulled short which creates a thicker beverage

Granita - A latte made with frozen milk

Iced Tea - Brewed tea, served chilled

Mochaccino - A cappuccino made with chocolate

Soy Latte - A latte made with soy milk, instead of milk

Coffee Roasters

Many cafes in this book obtain their coffee beans from local and international roasters and wholesale distributors listed below. If you're a true coffee enthusiast, or just want to have a better appreciation of what goes into the beverage you buy, these "name brand" firms are worth getting to know.

Caffe Vita
1005 East Pike Street
Seattle, WA 98122
206-709-4440
www.caffevita.com

In business since 1996, Caffe Vita distributes its roasted coffee beans and owns and operates a few retail stores in the Seattle area. Caffe Artigiano in Downtown Vancouver (check index) is the exclusive Canadian distributor.

Canterbury Coffee Corp.
22071 Fraserwood Way
Richmond, BC V6W 1J5
604-270-2326
www.canterburycoffee.com

Established in 1981, Canterbury roasts and distributes its coffee beans from its plant in Richmond to restaurants, supermarkets, gourmet stores and cafes.

Casa Del Caffe
1085 East Cordova Street
Vancouver, BC V6A 1M8
604-254-0354
www.casadelcaffe.com

Founded in Vancouver in 1981, Casa Del Caffe distributes its roasted beans to cafes and restaurants.

Coffee Roasters

Cuppa Joe Coffee Co.
104 - 350 East Kent Avenue South
Vancouver, BC V5X 4N6
604-709-4563
www.cuppajoecoffee.com

Established in 1999, this Vancouver roasting company distributes its beans to coffee bars, cafes, delis, grocery stores, offices, and organic home delivery services. The company owns a couple of 'Cuppa Joe' retail locations in Vancouver (check index).

Illy Espresso Canada Inc.
7370 Bramalea Road, Unit 23
Mississauga, ON L5S 1N6
905-673-6596
www.illy.com

Illy has roasted its brand of coffee beans in Trieste, Italy since 1933 and exports to over sixty countries.

Ionia S.p.A.
Via Trieste, 306 - 95100 Dagala del Re - S.Venerina, Italy
011 095/953006
www.ioniacaffe.it

The Ionia Coffee Company was founded in 1960 in Dagala del Re, Italy, and distributes its coffee in many countries throughout the world.

JJ Bean House of Coffee
1904 Powell Street
Vancouver, BC V5l 1J3
604-254-0161
www.jjbeancoffee.com

Founded in Vancouver, JJ Bean roasts its own coffee for distribution to cafes and restaurants, and operates a few retail stores in Vancouver (check index).

Coffee Roasters

Kicking Horse Coffee Co.
Box 2948
Invermere, BC V0A 1K0
250-342-4489
www.kickinghorsecoffee.com

The Kicking Horse Coffee Company is a micro roaster nestled in the Canadian Rockies from where it distributes its coffee beans to cafes in Canada.

Lavazza Premium Coffees Corp.
3 Park Avenue, 35th Floor
New York, NY 10016
212-725-8800
www.lavazza.com

Since 1895, Lavazza has been roasting its own beans in Italy and exporting them worldwide.

Milano Coffee Roasting Co.
156 West 8th Avenue
Vancouver, BC V5L 1N2
604-879-4468
www.coffeemilano.com

Established in Vancouver, Milano roasts and wholesales its coffee beans to many cafes and restaurants.

Coffee Roasters

Salt Spring Roasting Co.
211 Horel Road
Salt Spring Island, BC V8K 2A4
800-332-8858
www.saltspringroasting.com

Salt Spring Roasting Co. roasts its organic coffee beans at its facility on Salt Spring Island from where the beans are distributed wholesale to cafes all over. The company operates two cafes on Salt Spring Island (check index).

Seattle's Best Coffee
300 - 970 Homer Street
Vancouver, BC V6A 2W7
604-685-8686
www.sbc.ca

Since 1968, Seattle's Best Coffee has been roasting its coffee beans in the Pacific Northwest. Besides operating its own cafes internationally, including Vancouver (check index), the company distributes its beans to restaurants, hotels, and colleges, among many other places.

Starbucks Coffee Company
128 West 6th Avenue
Vancouver, BC V5Y 1K6
604-708-9233
www.starbucks.com

Established in 1972 in Seattle, where the coffee beans are roasted. Starbucks distributes coffee, syrups and confections to its thousands of retail stores throughout Canada, USA and worldwide (check index for a 'sample' of Starbucks in our region). A few local independent cafes also feature Starbucks' brand.

Coffee Roasters

Torrefazione Italia Inc.
100 - 1737 West 3rd Avenue
Vancouver, BC V6J 1K7
604-738-7400
www.titalia.com

Since 1986, Torrefazione beans have been roasted in Seattle and distributed to cafes, restaurants and hotels internationally. Torrefazione Italia owns and operates its several cafes in the United States and Canada (check index).

Trees Organic Coffee
450 Granville Street
Vancouver, BC V6C 1V4
604-684-5060

Located in Vancouver, Trees roasts its own organic coffee beans at its store and distributes them to a select group of cafes in our region.

Yoka's Coffee & Honey
3171 West Broadway
Vancouver, BC V6K 2H2
604-738-0905

Yoka's has been roasting its coffee beans in Vancouver since 1983 and operates its own retail store in Vancouver's Kitsilano neighborhood (check index).

Theme Index

Art Exhibitions
Amy's Cake Shop	36
Anona Fine Foods	67
Café Vinifera	154
Expressohead Coffee House	48
Gallagher's Espresso Bar	111
Havana	69
Java Jasmine Coffeehouse	149
Portfolio Coffee Bar	25
Savary Island Pie Company	82
Solly's Bagelry	71
Torrefazione Italia	61, 82, 143
Turk's Coffee House	74
Whitby's Bookstore & Coffee House	123

Author Readings
Indigo Books Café	86
Starry Dynamo Café	72
Whitby's Bookstore & Coffee House	123

Bakeries
Amy's Cake Shop	36
Anona Fine Foods	67
Benny's Bagels	38
Boleto	40
Bread Garden Bakery & Cafe	11, 12, 41, 42, 43, 80, 84, 92, 93, 104, 110, 116, 122

165

Theme Index

Canadian Maple Delights	13
Calhoun's Bakery Cafe	45
Capers Community Market	45
Cascadia Wholefoods Bakery	140
Cravings Coffee & Bakery	116, 128 & 129
Ecco Il Pane	47
Java Cat Coffee	19, 20
La Petite France	52
Max's Bakery & Delicatessen	53, 54
Mount Royal Bagel Factory	86
The Naam	55
Panne Rizo Bakery Café	56
Savary Island Pie Company	82
Solly's Bagelry	57, 71
Terra Breads	59
Trees Organic Coffee	29
Uprising Breads Bakery	74
Urban Fare	29

Bookstores

Chapters	106, 118, 130, 143, 154
Characters Fine Books	46
Indigo Books Café	86
Virgin Megastore Cafe	30
Whitby's Bookstore & Coffee House	123
Wendel's Books & Cafe	131

Theme Index

Licensed

Benny's Bagels	38
Boleto	40
Café Crepe	12, 44
Café Vinifera	154
Caffe Artigiano	13
Craving on Bay	94
Fish Cafe	49
Havana	69
Indigo Books Café	86
Kino Café	51
Montmartre	70
Moonpennies	23
Myles of Beans	106
The Naam	55
Sophie's Cosmic Cafe	57
Tomato Fresh Food Café	60
Urban Fare	29

Live Music

Café Madeleine	44
Gallagher's Espresso Bar	111
Grab-a-Java	147
Havana	69
Higher Grounds	50
Indigo Books Café	86
Java Jasmine Coffeehouse	149
Jitters Coffee House	105

167

Theme Index

Kino Café	51
La Solace Café	52
The Lookout Coffee House	81
Montmartre	70
Myles of Beans	106
The Naam	55
Savary Island Pie Company	82
Secret Garden Tea Co.	124
Starry Dynamo Café	72
Torrefazione Italia	61, 82, 143
Trees Organic Coffee	29
Virgin Megastore Cafe	30
Urban Fare	29
Whitby's Bookstore & Coffee House	123

Poetry

Java Jasmine Coffeehouse	149
Mocambo Coffee	141
Montmartre	70
Myles of Beans	106
Savary Island Pie Company	82
Starry Dynamo Café	72
Sweet Tooth Cafe	72
Trees Organic Coffee	29
Whitby's Bookstore & Coffee House	123

Cafe Index

A

Abbruzzo Cappuccino Bar 66
Amy's Cake Shop 36
Anona Fine Foods 67
Aromaz 8
Artistico Greek Cafe 66
Auntie Em's Kitchen 134

B

Bean Around The World Coffees 36, 140
Bean Bros. 37
Benny's Bagels 38
Big Dog Deli 8
Big Joe Coffee 9
Blenz Coffee 39
Blinding Light Cinema & Café 9
Blue Parrot Espresso Bar 39, 40
Bojangles Café 10
Bojangles on the Waterfront 10
Boleto 40
Brass & Beans 92
Bread Garden 11, 12, 41, 42, 43, 80, 84, 92, 93, 104, 110, 116, 122
The Butler Did It 43

C

Café Amore 104
Café Crepe 12, 44
Café Madeleine 44
Café Vinifera 154
Caffe Artigiano 13
Caffe Calabria 67
Calhoun's Bakery Cafe 45
Canadian Maple Delights 13
Capers Community Market 45
Cascadia Wholefoods Bakery 140
Characters Fine Books 46
Citrus Café 14
Chef Bernard's Café 134
Clancy's Tea Cosy 124
Coo Coo Coffee 14
Cove Fine Foods 80
Craving on Bay 94
Cravings Coffee & Bakery 116, 128, 129
Cuppa Joe Coffee Co. 68

D

Death By Chocolate 15, 46, 94, 105, 111, 135
Death By Chocolate Express 16
Delany's 16, 81, 85
Demitasse Coffeebar 141

E

Ecco Il Panne 47
The Elysian Room 47
Epicurean Delicatessen 48
Esquires Coffee House 117
Expressohead Coffee House 48

F

Fish Café 49

G

Gallagher's Espresso Bar 111
Gallery Café 17
Garibaldi's Espresso 85
Ghirardelli Soda Fountain 17
Grab-a-Java 147
Granville Island Coffee House 49

169

Cafe Index

The Grind & Gallery 68
Grounds For Appeal 18
Guttenberg's Café 18

H

Havana 69
Higher Grounds 50
Hole In The Wall 19

I

Indigo Books Café 86

J

Java Cat Coffee 19, 20
Java Expressions 153
Java Hut Espresso Co. 50, 118
Java Jasmine Coffeehouse 149
Jitters Coffee House 105
JJ Bean House of Coffee 51, 70
The Junction Magazine & Coffee House 117

K

Kino Café 51

L

La Petite France 52
La Solace Cafe 52
Lingo Cyberbistro 20
The Lookout Coffee House 81
Lugz Coffee Lounge 69

M

Mario's Coffee Express 21
Max's Bakery & Delicatessen 53, 54
Meinhardt Fine Foods 54
Mocambo Coffee 141
Mondo Gelato 21
Montmartre 70
Moon Beans Coffee Café 22
Moonpennies 23
Mount Royal Bagel Factory 86
Mum's Gelati 24, 55
Myles Of Beans Coffee House 106

N

The Naam 55

P

Panne Rizo Bakery Café 56
Pia's Classic Kaffe 24
Portfolio Coffee Bar 25
Portobello 135

S

Salt Spring Roasting Co. 150, 151
Savary Island Pie Company 82
Seattle's Best Coffee 25, 56
Secret Garden Tea Co. 124
Solly's Bagelry 57, 71
Sophie's Cosmic Cafe 57
Starbucks 26, 27, 28, 58, 71, 87, 95, 96, 98, 99, 106, 112, 118, 119, 122, 123, 130, 136, 142, 143, 149, 154, 155
Starry Dynamo Café 72
Sweet Tooth Cafe 72

T

T 125
Terra Breads 59

Cafe Index

Tomato Fresh Food Café 60
Tony's Coffee 60
Tony's Deli 73
Torrefazione Coloiera 73
Torrefazione Italia 61, 82, 143
Trees Organic Coffee 29
Truffles Bistro 61
Turk's Coffee House 74

U

Uprising Breads Bakery 74
Urban Fare 29

V

Virgin Megastore Cafe 30

W

Wendel's Books & Cafe 131
Whitby's Bookstore & Coffee House 123

Y

Yaletown Market 30
Yoka's Coffee & Honey 62

The Final Word

There is absolutely no paid advertising in this book, and no cafe paid to be included in these pages. The authors chose all cafes in this publication for their uniqueness, positive attributes, and neighborhood popularity.

That said, if you know of a cafe in southwestern British Columbia that you feel deserves mention in a subsequent edition of **CAFES Vancouver**, share your views! The authors can be reached by e-mail at **feedback@cafesvancouver.com**.

Although the authors cannot promise they will be included, all suggestions will receive due consideration.

Continue your exploration of Vancouver's local and regional cafe culture by visiting **www.cafesvancouver.com**. While not the final word on the subject, it's a great place to start!

Notes

Notes

Notes